TITANIC

SHIPWRECKS AND
SUNKEN TREASURE

TITANIC

SHIPWRECKS AND
SUNKEN TREASURE

By
John Malam

Consultant
Angus Konstam

A Dorling Kindersley Book

Dorling  Kindersley

LONDON, NEW YORK, MUNICH,
MELBOURNE, and DELHI

Project Editor Margaret Hynes
Project Art Editor Keith Davis
Senior Editor Fran Jones
Senior Art Editor Stefan Podhorodecki
Category Publisher Linda Martin
Managing Art Editor Jane Thomas
Picture Researcher Jo de Gray
DK Picture Library Jonathan Brooks
Production Jenny Jacoby
DTP Designer Siu Yin Ho

First published in Great Britain in 2003 by
Dorling Kindersley Limited
80 Strand, London WC2R 0RL

A Penguin Company

4 6 8 10 9 7 5 3

The CIP Catalogue record for this book is available
from the British Library

ISBN 0-7513-3756-0

Reproduced by Colourscan, Singapore
Printed and bound by L.E.G.O., Italy

To contact the author, write to johnmalam@aol.com

See our complete
catalogue at
www.dk.com

CONTENTS

6
INTRODUCTION

8
PERILS OF THE SEA

14
SHIPWRECK SEEKERS

20
TITANIC TRAGEDY

30
TREASURE HUNT

40
THE GELDERMALSEN

46
WRECKED WARSHIPS

56
RAISING THE VASA

63
PLUNDERING PIRATES

68
LOST LINERS

76
SURVIVORS' STORIES

82
ALL WASHED UP!

85
REFERENCE SECTION

94
INDEX

96
CREDITS

INTRODUCTION

In the excitement that surrounded the launch of the luxury liner *Titanic*, there were many who believed she was an unsinkable ship. Just four days into her one and only voyage, the unthinkable happened, and she plunged to the seabed. The truth is, there's no such thing as an unsinkable ship, a fact learned over and over again, ever since the first vessel dared to cross the sea – and didn't come home.

The seabed is littered with an unknown number of ships, each of them a shipwreck, whose final journey ended in disaster. Every one has a story to tell, but not every story can be told. For each wreck whose resting place is known, there are countless thousands of ships whose graves have never been found. These are the world's lost ships – ships taken by the sea, ships the sea still hides, ships whose stories have no end.

SHIPWRECKS ARE FULL OF RICHES – NOT JUST VALUABLE OBJECTS, BUT IMPORTANT AND UNIQUE EVIDENCE ABOUT HISTORY.

There are people who spend their whole lives searching for shipwrecks. While some are salvors who recover cargo and fittings, and sometimes even the ship itself, others are treasure-hunters hoping to strike it rich. Then there are historians and archaeologists, for whom a shipwreck is a time capsule whose lid was closed the day the ship was lost. For them, a shipwreck, and all that it conceals, is treasure of another kind – an underwater Tutankhamun's tomb.

The shipwrecks described in this book are from many periods in history, and are of many different types, from ancient wooden merchant ships to modern steel warships. The sea claimed them, and the sea has preserved them. Those who sailed in them knew them as living, working vessels. We know them only as doomed ships: shipwrecks.

For those who want to explore the subject in greater detail, there are Log On "bites" that appear throughout the book. These will direct you to websites where you can check out even more about shipwrecks. So, *bon voyage* – have a good journey!

John Malam

PERILS OF THE SEA

The sea is a dangerous place and nowhere is completely safe for a ship to sail. Even ships considered "unsinkable", such as the *Titanic*, have been wrecked. Sailors of today, like ancient mariners, watch out for perils that could send their ships on a voyage to the bottom of the sea, but sometimes they create dangers for themselves through human error.

Beneath the waves

Submerged beneath the rough waters of the North Sea, about 6.5 km (4 miles) from the coast of the Netherlands, is the wreck of HMS *Lutine*, a 32-gun wooden warship of the British Navy. She sailed for the Netherlands on 9 October 1799, where she was to deliver a cargo of gold and silver bullion to British soldiers stationed there. It never reached them, for in the early hours of 10 October, the *Lutine* struck a sandbank, broke up, and sank to the seabed.

The official explanation, given at the time of the disaster, said that the ship foundered in bad weather. However, some of today's historians think this was a cover-up story. It's true there was a storm blowing that night, but they find it hard to understand how a naval ship in good condition, and with a

WEIRD WORLD

MENTION "DAVY JONES' LOCKER" TO A SAILOR AND IT'LL SEND SHIVERS DOWN HIS SPINE. IT'S A SAILOR'S TERM FOR THE BOTTOM OF THE SEA, THE FINAL DESTINATION OF DROWNED MEN AND LOST SHIPS.

skilled crew, could have been wrecked when others were not. They wonder if someone on board misread a chart, or made a mistake when calculating her position. If so, then it was human error that sent the *Lutine* too close to land.

Out of 270 men, only Able Seaman John Rogers survived, and 1,900 gold bars, 500 silver bars, and thousands of gold and silver coins were lost. The treasure was valued at £1.2 million (about £40 million in today's money) and salvage work on the wreck began at once. It has continued on and off to the present day. Even after 200 years there's still plenty of treasure to be found.

The Lutine Bell

It's not the missing gold that *HMS Lutine* is best known for – it's her bronze bell, dredged up in 1858. It hangs inside the Lloyd's Building, London, which is where ship-owners from around the world go to insure ships and cargoes against the perils of the sea. Until 1979 the Lutine Bell was rung once each time a ship was lost, its sad chime echoing around the building. Although it is now only rung when important announcements are to be made,

it is still seen as a symbol of the perils faced by ships at sea.

Human error

All humans make mistakes at some time, and it's thought that as many as eight out of every ten ships are damaged – or wrecked – because of human error. If a sailor makes a mistake when plotting the course of his ship, he could send her onto rocks. If his charts are out of date, he won't know if there are new sandbanks to avoid. If a stevedore (a cargo handler) hasn't secured the cargo, the load could shift, causing the ship to tilt.

Even a mistake made when a ship is being built can cause an accident. For instance, a welder might use a weak weld to join the steel plates of the hull together. Years later the weld could rip apart, letting sea water pour in.

ALTHOUGH THE SEA COVERS ABOUT TWO-THIRDS OF THE EARTH'S SURFACE, MANY SHIPS HAVE ENDED THEIR DAYS SMASHED AGAINST ROCKY COASTS.

Natural causes

Among the greatest perils ships encounter are the ones thrown at them by nature. Strong winds can whip up ocean waves of alarming size. These enormous waves usually damage a ship at sea by swamping it with water, rather than tipping it over. Hurricanes (gigantic tropical storms) bring torrential rains, winds as fast as 240 kmh (150 mph), and mountainous seas. Some are powerful enough to pick up

North and South Poles. They became trapped during winter when the ice grows, as more sea water freezes to form pack ice (large masses of floating ice). The pressure of this ice saw the end of many wooden-hulled ships. It crushed them in its vice-like grip until timbers snapped and water poured in. Today, ice is more likely to be

THERE ARE ON AVERAGE SIX ATLANTIC HURRICANES EACH YEAR

boats and throw them onto land. Thick sea fog, formed when warm air blows across cold ocean water, can cause a ship to lose its way and run aground, or collide with another vessel.

In shallow water, banks of sand can easily capture a ship as the tide goes out. Currents move sandbanks, so a boat's charts can only indicate roughly where they lie. In the past, some ships found themselves stranded near the ice-bound areas around the

A GIANT WAVE ROLLS THE FISHING BOAT, *THE ANDREA GAIL* OVER IN THE 2000 HOLLYWOOD FILM, *THE PERFECT STORM.*

involved in accidents when it drifts into shipping lanes in the form of icebergs. This was the case for the *Titanic*, which was sunk by an iceberg in 1912.

According to the vivid imaginations of sailors, writers, and film studios, there are giant sea monsters – sharks and whales that head-butt or bite holes through the sides of ships.

Enemy action

Other dangers are of our own making, but in times of war it's a case of sink an enemy ship before she sinks you. Mines loaded with explosives lie in wait for a ship to hit them, torpedoes are fired by submarines and dropped from planes, and destroyers (an appropriate name for a

SEA BATTLES BETWEEN SAILING SHIPS WERE FOUGHT AT CLOSE RANGE. MODERN WARSHIPS FIGHT AT LONG RANGE.

battleship) fire high-explosive shells at the enemy. Even in peacetime a ship can fall victim to enemy attack. Pirates might board it, steal its cargo, then sink it, in an attempt to hide the evidence of their crime.

Mysterious forces

Sometimes a ship is lost for no obvious reason. When this happens all sorts of rumours can start up about what might – or might not – have happened to her. Take, for example, the patch of Atlantic Ocean between Bermuda, Puerto Rico, and the Florida coastline of the USA. Within this triangular area ships (and planes) have been known to vanish without trace, and there are plenty of people who believe that mysterious forces are at work.

Lots of theories exist, from giant bubbles of methane gas (the stinky stuff that smells of bad eggs) floating up from the seabed and capsizing ships, to ships being plucked from the water by aliens. Now what use is a ship to super-intelligent aliens? Some people, however, believe the lost ships are no more than unfortunate victims of human

WEIRD WORLD
NO ONE KNOWS WHAT HAPPENED TO THE 10 PEOPLE ON BOARD THE *MARY CELESTE*, AN AMERICAN SHIP FOUND ABANDONED IN THE MIDDLE OF THE ATLANTIC OCEAN IN 1872.

error, or the storms and rough seas for which the so-called Bermuda Triangle is notorious. You'll have to decide for yourself what you believe!

One thing about the Bermuda Triangle is certain. Ever since records began, way back in 1780 when American warships *General Gates* and *Saratoga* vanished, thousands of ships, big and small, have sailed into the area, but have not sailed out again. Who knows, maybe they are still there, trapped in a time warp. You're welcome to go and search for them – if you dare!

NATURAL PHENOMENA, SUCH AS WHIRLPOOLS, MAY BE RESPONSIBLE FOR THE DISAPPEARANCE OF SHIPS.

LOG ON...
Find out more at:
www.bermuda-triangle.org

SHIPWRECK SEEKERS

Valuable cargoes have always lured divers to sunken wrecks. But in the past, some wrecks were just too deep and inaccessible. Developments in diving and salvage technology, however, mean that wrecks are now reached at greater depths than ever before. Scientists and salvage experts can locate and map sites without ever having to get their feet wet.

WRECK-HUNTER DR ROBERT BALLARD AND HIS TEAM USE CHARTS AND SCANNERS TO FIND THE *TITANIC*.

Locating a wreck

After a ship has sunk all that might be left on the surface are its passengers and crew (dead and alive), and floating wreckage known as flotsam. These are often the only signs of a tragedy, and this evidence may drift far from the scene of the accident carried by waves and wind. Locating the wreck can be like looking for a needle in a haystack – you know it's there, but where?

If the missing ship is a modern one, coastguards can give searchers its last known position. If, however, it's an old ship, then wreck-hunters work as detectives. They can spend months, and even years, sifting through old documents and examining maps and charts, following a trail of clues that might lead them to a wreck. Wreck-hunting is a painstaking business, and no one wants to waste time or money looking in the wrong place. Only by swimming down to the seabed, scanning it with sound waves (SONAR), or by using submersible vehicles equipped with lights and cameras will

MANY MYSTERIES OF THE PAST CAN BE UNLOCKED THROUGH THE STUDY OF SHIPWRECKS FOUND ON THE SEABED.

WEIRD WORLD
THE UNDERWATER BREATHING
TUBE KNOWN AS A *SNORKEL*
GETS ITS NAME FROM THE
GERMAN WORD *SCHNORKEL*,
WHICH IS A REFERENCE
TO THE SNORING
NOISE IT MAKES.

JOHN LETHBRIDGE BUILT ONE OF THE FIRST PRACTICAL DIVING BELLS IN 1715.

information about past times. Either way, someone – or something – has got to dive down to the wreck.

If you think diving is new, think again. As long ago as 480 BC a man named Scyllias, described as "the most expert diver of his day", dived to the bottom of

THE FREEDOM OF MOVEMENT PROVIDED BY THE AQUALUNG HELPS ARCHAEOLOGISTS TO PERFORM DELICATE EXCAVATION WORK.

the presence of a shipwreck be confirmed.

A wreck can also be found by luck. Pleasure divers, tourists on a beach at low tide, and fishermen whose nets snag on a submerged object, or even bring something to the surface, stand just as much chance of finding a wreck as a salvage expert or a scientist.

E arly diving

Once a shipwreck has been located, it's time to decide what course of action to take, and that all depends on what sort of vessel it is, and how old it is. A modern wreck might need to be examined to discover what caused it to sink, whereas an ancient wreck can provide

the Aegean Sea to grab treasure from Persian wrecks. Scyllias is the world's first-known salvor – a person who salvages cargo. Today's salvors, under the time-honoured law of salvage, keep a percentage of the goodies for themselves, just as Scyllias did.

It's the prospect of finding treasure that has led divers to experiment with diving devices. Scyllias, like the sponge divers of his day, could probably only hold his breath for three or four minutes. It wasn't until 2,000 years later, in the 1500s, that divers learned how to stay down for longer periods. They

It was made from thick, watertight fabric, and was weighed down by lead weights. Over their heads, divers wore metal helmets. An air hose and safety line linked the diver to a surface ship. There, a crew member used a pump to force air down the hose into the diver's helmet. The safety line was used for sending simple signals to the ship.

LOG ON...
For the history of diving:
www.divingheritage.com

IN 1837, GERMAN INVENTOR AUGUSTUS SIEBE INVENTED THE FIRST REAL DIVING SUIT.

descended inside "diving bells" – wooden barrels containing a supply of trapped air. Later, fresh air was pumped into the bells through a tube. This helped to prolong dive times.

It wasn't until 1837, however, that divers could leave their diving bells and go for a walk on the seabed, thanks to the invention of the diver's suit.

Able to descend to 50 m (165 ft), this was the start of modern diving and salvage.

The latest diving equipment

Today's divers have all the advantages of modern technology. In shallow water they swim freely in lightweight rubber wetsuits, breathing oxygen from cylinders strapped to their backs known as aqualungs (underwater lungs). Wetsuit divers can descend to a depth of around 100 m (330 ft) – any deeper and the diver must be sealed inside an atmospheric diving suit (ADS). It's a bulky, rigid suit that protects its operator from the dangerous effects of water pressure. A diver wearing an ADS can work at depths of up to 610 m (2,000 ft) for almost six hours at a time.

Underwater vehicles

For wrecks that are so deep that divers cannot reach them, submersible vehicles are used. Some are manned, and can stay under water for up to 10 hours. Others are unmanned remotely operated vehicles (ROVs), controlled by operators from a mother ship on the surface. They can stay down even longer than manned submersibles. Automated

THE CREWS OF SUBMERSIBLES LIKE THIS ONE RELY ON THE LATEST COMPUTER WIZARDRY TO HELP THEM FIND THEIR WAY IN PITCH-BLACK WATERS.

ALVAGE WORK OFTEN INVOLVES USING
MECHANICAL RATHER THAN HI-TECH
EQUIPMENT TO RAISE SUNKEN SHIPS.

underwater vehicles (AUVs) are the most modern submersibles. Robots with artificial intelligence, they can remain under water for several months.

Wreck recovery

When archaeologists and accident investigators find wrecks, they sometimes decide to raise them for detailed investigation. It is just as important, however, to record where each object rested on the seabed, as this sort of information can tell a lot about what happened to the ship. So divers spend much of their time under water measuring, mapping, sketching, and taking photographs. Once they have recorded the area, lighter objects are raised with the help of an airlift – a buoyant, air-filled bag. Salvage vessels fitted with cranes are used to raise the wreck to the surface. The ship and its various artefacts are then cleaned and studied, and later they may be put on display in museums.

WEIRD WORLD

SALVORS UNDERESTIMATED THE WEIGHT OF THE GUNBOAT USS CAIRO WHEN THEY RAISED IT IN 1964. THEIR CABLES SLICED THE HULL TO PIECES, AND THE VESSEL'S ARMOUR FELL BACK INTO THE WATER.

TITANIC TRAGEDY

In 1907, Bruce Ismay, the managing director of the White Star Line shipping company, and Lord William Pirrie of Harland and Wolff shipbuilders, devised a plan to build a lavish transatlantic liner. She was to be the largest and most luxurious ship ever to float on water. Within four years their ship, which they called the *Titanic*, was ready to be launched, and before she departed for her maiden voyage, her proud builders boasted that she was "virtually unsinkable".

The *Titanic* is launched

On Wednesday morning, 31 May, 1911, thousands of people lined the banks of the River Lagan, Belfast, Ireland, to watch the launch of the *Titanic*. It had taken a team of metal-bashers just two years to construct the ship's massive body. As her 269 m- (883 ft-) long hull grew, fashioned from sheets of steel held together by three million rivets, the ship began to attract public

attention and became the talk of the town.

It was not the custom at Harland and Wolff to have ship-naming ceremonies, so the *Titanic* did not have a bottle of champagne smashed in celebration across her bow. Instead, shortly after midday, two rockets were fired into the sky, followed by a third five minutes later. This shot signalled that the 26,000-tonne hull was about to slide down the greased slipway. As the ship began to move, the crowds along the river cheered, tug boats blew their whistles, and 62 seconds later the *Titanic* was afloat in Belfast harbour.

A floating palace

The *Titanic* was launched as an empty shell, so once she was in the water, she was manoeuvred by tug boats to a fitting-out berth. It was here that her four funnels were put in place, and far below them, at the very bottom of the ship, 29 boilers and 159 furnaces were installed to provide steam power for her engines. While engineers worked below deck, carpenters, and decorators prepared the passengers' cabins and the ship's public areas. Her builders ensured that she had the best of everything. She had a fitness gym and a swimming pool (she was the first ship to have one), a hospital, and a library. Her wireless room contained the most up-to-date radio communication equipment, and electricity surged through

THE *TITANIC* WAS A SPLENDID SIGHT AS SHE STEAMED THROUGH THE WATER. AT NIGHT SHE SHONE FROM END TO END, ILLUMINATED BY HER CABIN LIGHTS.

WHITE STAR
ROYAL MAIL STEAMER
"TITANIC"

WEIRD WORLD
THE *TITANIC*'S ENORMOUS CENTRAL
ANCHOR WAS THE BIGGEST OF THE
SHIP'S THREE ANCHORS. IT TOOK
A TEAM OF 20 HORSES TO HAUL
THE LOAD TO THE HARLAND
AND WOLFF SHIPYARD,
READY FOR INSTALLATION
ON THE DECK.

320 km (200 miles) of wiring, bringing light to her 10,000 lightbulbs. No expense was spared, and at £1.5 million ($7.5 million) she was the most expensive ship of her day. At today's prices this is about £80 million ($400 million).

Built to last

Harland and Wolff were proud of the ship they had built, and they were confident that their design and workmanship was second to none. In fact, the shipyard claimed that the *Titanic* was "virtually unsinkable". They felt they could say this because inside the ship's hull were 15 watertight bulkheads (tall steel walls) which divided the ship into 16 compartments. If an accident did happen, said the builders, the ship would stay afloat even if four of the compartments flooded.

However, there was a problem with the design of the bulkheads and they did not go all the way to the top of the hull. Instead, there was a gap at the top of each one. Therefore, if water completely filled one compartment, it would spill over the gap and flood the next compartment. The same thing would happen in that compartment, and the next, and so on until all 16 were flooded. During the construction phase, no one seems to have thought that the gaps mattered, and work continued for the first voyage.

The sheer bulk and solidity of the *Titanic* meant that people soon dropped the word "virtually" from Harland and Wolff's statement, and many people began to believe that the ship was truly unsinkable.

The voyage begins

On 3 April, 1912, the *Titanic* sailed into Southampton, on

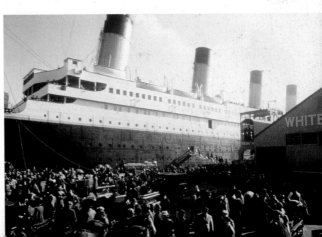

THE *TITANIC'S*
ROUTE TOOK HER ACROSS THE
ENGLISH CHANNEL TO FRANCE, OVER THE
IRISH SEA TO IRELAND, AND THEN ACROSS
THE ATLANTIC OCEAN FOR NEW YORK.

the south coast of England.
This was to be her home port,
from where her voyages to
New York, USA, would start.
For the next week she was
stocked with supplies, including
34,000 kg (75,000 lb) meat;
5,000 kg (11,000 lb) fish;
40,000 hens' eggs; 40 tonnes
potatoes; 800 bundles
asparagus; 7,000 lettuces;
795 kg (1,750 lb) ice cream;
36,000 apples; huge quantities
of milk and cream, tea and
coffee, beer and wine; 57,600
cups, saucers, bowls, and plates;
44,000 pieces of cutlery;
thousands of
tablecloths,
towels, blankets,
and sheets;
3,364 bags of
mail and 4,427
tonnes of coal.
  Shortly after
midday, April 10,
the *Titanic* left
Southampton, and

her first voyage was underway.
After brief stops at Cherbourg,
France, and Queenstown (now
Cobh) on the south coast of
Ireland, she steamed away from
Europe and into the emptiness
of the North Atlantic Ocean.
On board was her crew of
899 men and women, under
Captain Edward Smith, and
1,324 passengers. Some
travellers were rich and enjoyed
the luxury of first-class travel,
but most were poor folk with
cheap tickets who travelled
third class, taking with them
dreams of starting new lives on
the other side of the ocean.

The *Titanic* dream ends

  On 14 April,
after four days at
sea, their dreams
came to a tragic
end. For most
of that day the
Titanic's wireless
operators had
received messages
from nearby ships
warning her to

> ### WEIRD WORLD
> UP TO 15,000 ICEBERGS
> BREAK OFF FROM GLACIERS ON
> THE ICE-COVERED ISLAND OF
> GREENLAND EVERY YEAR, BUT
> FEWER THAN 500 OF THEM
> DRIFT AS FAR SOUTH AS THE
> NORTH ATLANTIC OCEAN
> SHIPPING LANES.

watch out for icebergs. Then, as midnight approached, one of the *Titanic's* lookouts, Frederick Fleet, called out the words feared by every sailor: "Iceberg, right ahead!" But a collision could not be avoided. The great liner's starboard (right) side scraped against the ice mountain for 10 seconds, splitting her hull open below the waterline for a distance of 76 m (250 ft). Nothing could stop the sea from pouring into the ship. Nothing could prevent the ship's compartments from flooding. Nothing could halt the water from flowing over the tops of the bulkheads, and nothing could save the ship from sinking.

The death of a giant

It took about two-and-a-half hours for the *Titanic* to sink. As her bow dipped deeper into the icy sea, lifeboats were launched, but there weren't enough to hold all of the 2,223 people on board the stricken ship. Despite this fact, many lifeboats went into the sea with spaces to fill. They could have held more people, but they didn't. Morse Code distress signals were sent out by the ship's wireless operators (it was the first time the famous

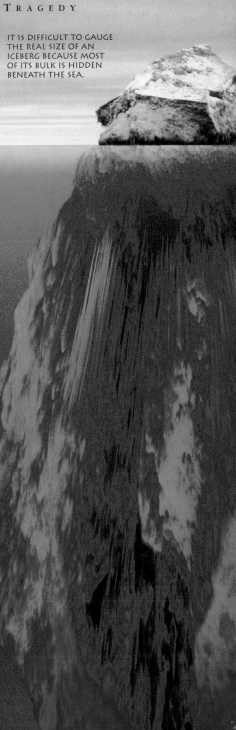

IT IS DIFFICULT TO GAUGE THE REAL SIZE OF AN ICEBERG BECAUSE MOST OF ITS BULK IS HIDDEN BENEATH THE SEA.

ONE OF THE SCENES IN THE FILM, *TITANIC*, SHOWED HOW SOME PEOPLE JUMPED SHIP AS THE FINAL LIFEBOATS WERE LOWERED.

SOS signal was ever used), and flares were fired.

By 2.18 am the *Titanic* was vertical. Her propellers were out of the water, held high into the night sky. Her lights went out, and moments later she broke into two pieces. First to sink was the bow section. It was shortly followed by the stern. The *Titanic's* shattered body fell to the seabed, 3.8 km (2.3 miles) below the surface and 1,517 people lost their lives. Captain Smith went down with his ship. Frederick Fleet lived to tell his story.

F ind the *Titanic*!
Immediately after the disaster, people talked about recovering the *Titanic*, but even if she had been located, the technology to

LOG ON...

www.titanic-titanic.com
www.encyclopedia-titanica.org

were not developed until the late 1970s. It was then that the search for the wreck really began. Many of those who went in search of the *Titanic* hoped to be the first wreck-hunter to find the world's most famous lost ship. Everybody was curious to know if the sunken wreck would still show signs of her original splendour.

One of those to hunt for the wreck was an American marine geologist, Dr Robert Ballard. His working life involved exploring the hidden depths of the ocean with submersible vehicles. He'd been thinking about searching for the *Titanic* for 12 years before the summer of 1985, when he led an American/French expedition to find her.

Over the course of five weeks, Ballard's research ships, *Le Suroit* and the *Knorr*, surveyed more than 260 sq km (100 sq miles) of Atlantic seabed using

reach her was not available. The *Titanic* sank in extremely deep water about 800 km (500 miles) off the coast of Newfoundland, Canada. The tools necessary for such a large-scale operation in deep waters

TITANIC
DISASTER
GREAT LOSS
OF LIFE
EVENING NEWS

IN THE ABSENCE OF NEWS FROM
THE WHITE STAR LINE, WORRIED
RELATIVES SCOURED NEWSPAPERS FOR
INFORMATION ABOUT LOVED ONES.

sonar and an unmanned submersible called *Argo*.
At 1 am, on 1 September, 1985, *Argo* relayed a curious image to its surface vessel. It was a view of one of the *Titanic*'s boilers. Ballard's team had found the wreck!

THIS CHERUB WAS PART OF THE FIRST-CLASS AFT GRAND STAIRCASE. MADE OF COPPER, ITS DESIGN IS INSPIRED BY 17TH-CENTURY PIECES.

The *Titanic* today

Dr Ballard gave the *Titanic* back to the world. For 73 years her location had been a mystery, and her discovery aroused massive worldwide interest.

Since 1985 there have been many expeditions to the wreck site. Some have gone there to study the wreck and the surrounding area in great detail, mapping it in the same ways as an archaeological site, which, in a way, it is. This work has helped us to understand where the iceberg struck, how much damage the collision caused, and what happened as the ship broke in two. Other

THE BOW AND STERN LIE 600 M (1,970 FT) APART ON THE SEABED

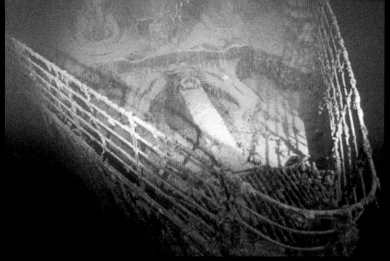

expeditions, however, have gone to the wreck to recover objects to put on display. More than 5,000 different items have been recovered, including personal possessions, nautical equipment, and some of the ship's fixtures and fittings. Even a 20-tonne piece of the ship's hull has been raised.

THE *TITANIC'S* BOW SANK FAST ENOUGH TO PLOUGH ITSELF MORE THAN 18 M (60 FT) DEEP INTO THE ATLANTIC SEABED.

Many people think it is wrong to recover items from the wreck, saying it is a grave that should be respected and left untouched. Other people believe that further exploration of the site may yield new discoveries among the twisted metal of the world's most famous shipwreck. What's certain is that with countless films, books, and websites to its name, the *Titanic* is now more famous than ever.

MODELMAKERS CREATED THIS RECONSTRUCTION OF THE *TITANIC'S* BOW FROM PHOTOGRAPHS AND VIDEO FOOTAGE TAKEN BY SUBMERSIBLES.

TREASURE HUNT

Imagine the excitement of discovering a shipwreck. Then imagine the even greater excitement of discovering that some, or all, of the wreck's cargo has survived. For salvors, marine archaeologists, and treasure-hunters, long-lost cargo is the ultimate underwater discovery, and they go to great efforts to recover it. Some recover the cargo for profit, while others study it, or put it on display in museums.

WRAPPED IN PAPER AND NEATLY STACKED IN BARRELS, THESE COINS WERE PART OF THE CARGO OF A WRECKED ENGLISH SHIP.

carried every imaginable kind of cargo. The riverboats of ancient Egypt returned from Punt (present-day Sudan and Eritrea) with gold, ebony (a black wood), elephant ivory, and living myrrh trees. The ships of the Greeks and Romans moved millions of pottery jars, filled with wine, cooking oil, and sauces, back and forth across the Mediterranean Sea, while others transported bronze and marble statues. Five and six hundred years ago the seas around China and Japan were the domain of junks – flat-bottomed trading ships – that carried porcelain pots from kiln

Hidden in the hold

Between the lower deck and the floor of a ship is a large open space called the hold. This is where cargo and ballast (heavy material that keeps a ship stable while it's at sea) are stowed. Ships have

A DIVER EMERGES FROM THE "GLASS WRECK", A VESSEL THAT SANK IN ABOUT 1025. HE'S HOLDING A GLASS FLASK, MADE IN SYRIA.

and other valuables. Some of these ships never reached their destinations. Their cargoes are out there right now, lost at sea, waiting for the day they'll be discovered and brought safely ashore.

Torpedoed treasure
During World War II (1939–45) many warships of the British Royal Navy acted as escorts. They protected merchant ships from Germany's "wolfpack" – her fleet of hunter-killer submarines, commonly known as U-boats (from *unterseeboot*, the German word for submarine). One such escort ship was HMS *Edinburgh*, whose mission in April 1942 was to guard a convoy of 13 merchantmen as they crossed from Murmansk, Russia, to Britain.

Shortly before the *Edinburgh* left the Russian port, 93 small wooden boxes were loaded into one of her bomb rooms. They contained 465 bars of gold, weighing 5 tonnes and valued at £1,547,080 ($2,320,620). It was to pay for goods sold to Russia by Britain, but it was to take almost 40 years for the

to market. The treasure fleets of Spain sailed in the 1600s loaded with gold, silver, and precious stones, and in more recent times ships have crossed the ocean carrying works of art

31

bullion to reach the safety of the shore. At dawn on April 30, the *Edinburgh* was attacked by the German submarine U-456, who fired two torpedoes into her. Two days later the crippled warship sank, and her valuable cargo went to the bottom of the icy Barents Sea, 245 m (800 ft) below the surface.

Salvage of the century

As the years passed the *Edinburgh*'s steel hull was

GOLD DOES NOT CORRODE OR RUST. EVEN AFTER DECADES OR CENTURIES AT SEA, IT STAYS BRIGHT.

attacked by rust, but the gold bars stayed as good as the day they were made, since gold does not tarnish. In fact, it increased in value, and by the late 1970s it was worth £45 million ($64 million).

The *Edinburgh* wreck lay in international waters, so even though the gold belonged to the British government, under the rules of salvage, the first salvor to recover the gold could claim a share of its value. Worse still, it could be pirated by a treasure-hunter who might keep the lot. The British government, concerned they might lose the gold, appointed a British salvage company, run by

Keith Jessop, to look for it. If Jessop salvaged the gold, then he and his backers could keep 45 per cent. The rest would be split between the British and Russian governments. If Jessop didn't recover it, he wouldn't be paid a thing. No one could even be certain the gold was there – it might have been blown to bits. Despite the risk of coming up empty-handed, Jessop went ahead.

In May 1981, Jessop and his team found the *Edinburgh*. That September, 12 divers, working in pairs, began to cut through the armour-plated hull. It took two weeks to reach the bomb room, where, amid piles of

THE BRITISH DELIBERATELY SANK THE DAMAGED *EDINBURGH*

ONCE THE GERMAN U-BOAT COMMANDER FIXED THE *EDINBURGH* IN HIS SIGHTS HE GAVE THE COMMAND TO FIRE.

unexploded shells, they found what they had come for – the boxes of Russian gold. Jessop salvaged 431 of the 465 bars, and after dividing them between all those who claimed a share, he was left with £2 million ($3 million) for himself – and gold bar number KP0620, the first bar brought to the surface. The remaining 34 bars were salvaged in 1986.

Diving into the past While the story of the *Edinburgh* reveals how modern-day salvors can become rich from their work, there are others who work below the

A DIVER LIFTS ONE OF THE COPPER INGOTS FROM THE ULUBURUN WRECK. EACH FOUR-HANDLED INGOT, IN THE SHAPE OF AN OX HIDE, WEIGHED ABOUT 27 KG (60 LB),

waves for the love of history, not financial reward. They know that whatever they find will not belong to them. They are the world's marine archaeologists, whose careful, painstaking work uncovers information about the past for us all to enjoy.

Over the centuries the jagged coastline of Turkey has caused the deaths of thousands of ships, driven onto its rocks by winds and waves. One wreck in particular has turned out to be

DATING FROM ABOUT 300 BC, THESE WINE AND OIL STORAGE JARS ARE DISPLAYED ON PIECES OF THE WRECKED SHIP FROM WHICH THEY CAME.

LOG ON...
Find out more at:
http://ina.tamu.edu/ub_main.htm

a treasure trove for archaeologists. It's known as the Uluburun wreck, after the cape in southern Turkey near where it came to grief in about 1300 BC. For almost 3,300 years it lay forgotten on the seabed, a mere 65 m (213 ft) from the shore, but 45 m (150 ft) below the surface. It all changed in 1982, when Turkish sponge diver Mehmet Çakir said that he had seen "metal biscuits with ears" at the bottom of the sea. The Turkish authorities thought Çakir's "biscuits" deserved investigating.

Copper cargo

A team led by George Bass, one of the world's leading marine archaeologists, and Turkish archaeologist Cemal Pulak undertook the search. They found that the biscuit-like objects were actually large, flat ingots of copper, each with four handles – the "ears". They discovered 475 big, heavy lumps of it, weighing about 10 tonnes. Doubtless it had been destined for workshops where, with the addition of tin, ancient metalworkers would have turned the copper into bronze tools and weapons.

However, the 15 m- (24 ft-) long merchant ship was carrying more than copper. For ten years, from 1984 to 1994, archaeologists dived 22,413 times to the wreck, spending a total of 6,613 hours on the site. Every part of it was carefully excavated so that nothing was missed, and thousands of objects were brought to the surface. Detailed plans were drawn and photographs were taken to build up a picture of what the cedar-wood ship looked like. It became clear that the Uluburun wreck was one of the oldest shipwrecks ever to be found.

A GOLD PENDANT WITH AN IMAGE OF A GODDESS WAS RECOVERED FROM THE ULUBURUN WRECK. IT MAY HAVE BEEN MADE IN SYRIA.

Treasure from many lands
The Uluburun wreck is thought to have started its journey somewhere in the eastern part of the Mediterranean Sea, and sailed westward. On board was a vast cargo of objects from 11 different lands. They included gold and silver jewellery from Canaan and Egypt, amber from the lands around the Baltic Sea, elephant tusks, ostrich eggshells, hippopotamus teeth, and ebony logs from Africa. There were cylinder seals from Mesopotamia (present-day Iran and Iraq), ingots of glass from Syria, ingots of tin, hundreds of pottery vases from Cyprus, and one tonne of resin.

Not only was the ship carrying a large and varied cargo, but it was an expensive one, perhaps even a royal offering from one ruler to another. The sinking of the ship would have been a disaster for its owners, but their loss is our gain, and much of the Uluburun wreck's treasure is now on display in the Bodrum Museum of Underwater Archaeology, Turkey.

Long lost loot
Not everything that comes up from the seabed goes into bank vaults (as the gold of the *Edinburgh* did), or into museums (as the objects from the Uluburun wreck did). There is another kind of searcher – a treasure-hunter. They split up their haul and sell it off.

IN ANCIENT TIMES HIPPOPOTAMUSES WERE HUNTED FOR THEIR TEETH – A VALUABLE SOURCE OF IVORY.

When a hurricane blew ships of the Spanish treasure fleet onto coral reefs off the Florida Keys, USA, in September 1622, an unimaginably valuable cargo of plundered riches was lost.

For some 40 years, between the 1580s and the 1620s, Spanish ships had sailed home to Europe in convoys, laden with loot taken from the peoples of Central and South America. Among the treasure ships was the *Nuestra Señora de Atocha*, a 500-tonne wooden galleon.

In 1622 she took on cargo at the ports of Cartagena, in present-day Colombia, and Portobello, in present-day Panama. Stowed away inside her hold were 161 ingots of gold, 901 ingots of silver, 250,000 silver coins, and a large quantity of uncut emeralds. The passengers who boarded her for the journey home were wealthy Spanish officials, merchants, and religious men, whose personal possessions included many objects of gold and silver studded with precious stones. When the *Atocha* sank, only five of the 265 people on board survived.

DIVER HERBERT HUMPHREY HOLDS UP IVORY TUSKS FOUND ON THE WRECK OF THE SPANISH SHIP *NUESTRA SEÑORA DE LAS MARAVILLAS*. THE SHIP WAS LOST OFF THE BAHAMAS IN 1656.

Going for gold

In the years that followed the disaster, Spanish salvors tried to locate the *Atocha*, but they never did. It was not until the 1970s that Mel Fisher, an American treasure-hunter, found traces of the wreck scattered over the seabed, and it was not until 1985 that he finally discovered the ship's priceless treasure. In that year, he recovered an impressive haul of silver coins, gold bars, and emeralds, together with silver bars, and chains and coins of gold. Fisher and his team eventually recovered much more. The *Atocha*'s cargo was the richest ever found. One jewel alone has been valued at over £1.2 million ($2 million).

THE *ATOCHA* YIELDED MUCH TREASURE, INCLUDING LENGTHS OF GOLD CHAIN AND GOLD CROSSES INLAID WITH EMERALDS.

display for the public to see.

Some of the treasure, such as the coins, has been sold to private collectors. Not everyone is happy with what has happened to the *Atocha*, especially archaeologists. They would have liked the vessel to have been carefully excavated and recorded, and all the finds kept together, not dispersed. Ultimately, salvors, marine archaeologists and treasure-hunters need to work closely together, just as their counterparts on land do.

IT TOOK MEL FISHER 16 YEARS TO FIND THE *ATOCHA'S* TREASURE

But it was not all plain sailing for Fisher. The State of Florida, who claimed the treasure was theirs, since it had been found within their territorial waters, took him to court. Eventually the courts decided Fisher was the owner, but he still gave Florida 20 per cent of what he had found, so it could go on

HERBERT HUMPHREYS WITH GOLD BARS RECOVERED FROM THE *NUESTRA SEÑORA DE LAS MARAVILLAS.*

THE GELDERMALSEN

Spare a moment for the china teacup, for it has a tale to tell. When tea became a fashionable drink among Europe's gentry in the 1600s, they wanted to sip it from the finest cups. European potters, however, could only make cups from heavy, dull pottery, so ships sailed to Asia to load up with vast quantities of shiny, white Chinese porcelain, called "Nanking" ware.

AMSTERDAM EMERGED AS A WORLD TRADING CENTRE IN THE 1600s. IT HAD DOZENS OF SHIPBUILDING YARDS INCLUDING THOSE OF THE DUTCH EAST INDIA COMPANY.

WEIRD WORLD
THE FIRST TEACUPS WERE ACTUALLY TEABOWLS – SMALL BOWLS WITHOUT HANDLES. WHEN EUROPEAN POTTERS STARTED MAKING TEAWARES, THEY COPIED THIS CHINESE SHAPE.

Trading places

In 1602, a group of traders in the Netherlands formed a single company known as the Verenigde Oostindische Compagnie (the VOC, or Dutch East India Company). The aim was to send ships to Asia to buy pepper, spices, indigo dye, porcelain, tropical hardwood, and other goods, all of which were desired in Europe. During the 200 years the company was in existence, it built around 1,500 ships that made some 5,000 journeys to Asia. Almost 650 of them came to grief, taking their crews and cargoes to the bottom of the sea. One of them was the *Geldermalsen*.

Load lugger

Built in 1746, the *Geldermalsen* was a large merchant ship measuring 45 m (150 ft) from prow to stern, and with a deep, wide hold for hundreds of tonnes of cargo. In 1748 she began her maiden voyage, sailing from the Netherlands, around Africa, and into the Indian Ocean, bound for the Dutch East India Company's trading posts in India, Java, and China. For two years she travelled the seaways of the

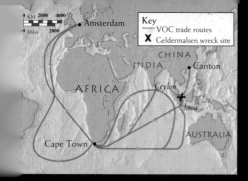

South China Sea, moving goods to and from the company's warehouses. In 1751 she sailed to Canton (present-day Guangzhou), a major port on the south coast of China, where she was loaded with cargo for Europe. Into her great hold, packed safely inside wooden crates, went 311,200 kg (306 tons) of tea, 147 bars of gold, silks, spices, lacquerware, and almost a quarter of a million pieces of Chinese porcelain.

According to the ship's manifest – her cargo list – teacups and saucers accounted for the greatest number of her precious pots – a sure sign of how popular tea-drinking had become in Europe.

Pirates were a menace, and to fight them off the

Geldermalsen was armed with 26 cannons, 100 hand grenades, rifles, swords, and gunpowder, but she didn't need them. On 3 January, 1752, a few days into her homeward voyage, human error caused her to strike a reef and sink. Of the 112 people on board, 80 drowned.

Change of name

For 233 years the ship lay undiscovered at the bottom of the South China Sea. As her cargo crates rotted their contents slowly spilled out, and tonnes of tea leaves floated down onto the porcelain pots,

Inventory of Porcelain

63,623 teacups and saucers
19,535 coffee cups and saucers
9,735 chocolate cups and saucers
578 tea pots, 548 milk jugs, 821 mugs
14,315 flat dinner plates
1,452 soup plates
75 fish bowls, 447 single dishes
1,000 nests of round dishes
195 butter dishes
2,563 bowls with saucers
25,921 slop bowls, 606 vomit pots
171 dinner services

blanketing them in a thick layer of soft material that protected them from the ravages of time. Then, in 1985, the wreck was found. As the full extent of the *Geldermalsen*'s cargo of crockery became known, she was given a nickname that has stuck: the "Nanking Cargo Wreck", after the town where it was once mistakenly thought Chinese porcelain was made.

WEIRD WORLD
AN ENGLISH FAMILY NAMED BLAKE, WHOSE MOTTO WAS "THINK AND THANK" IS SAID TO HAVE BEEN SENT A DINNER SERVICE FROM CHINA. THE POTTER MISREAD THE MOTTO AND WROTE "STINK AND STANK" ON EVERY PIECE.

It was actually made at Jingdezhen (present-day Fowliang), and was shipped to Europe from the port of Nanking (present-day Nanjing). As a result of this mix-up, European merchants called Chinese export porcelain "Nanking" ware.

This was the reason why

AMAZINGLY, EVEN THE MOST FRAGILE OBJECTS, SUCH AS THESE BOWLS AND THE *GELDERMALSEN'S* PORCELAIN, CAN SURVIVE A SHIP-WRECKING INCIDENT.

USING A METAL DETECTOR, SALVAGE LEADER MICHAEL HATCHER SEARCHES FOR METAL NEAR WHERE THE *GELDERMALSEN'S* MAIN ANCHOR WAS FOUND.

this name was used when referring to the pots that surfaced in the mid-1980s.

Hatcher's haul

The *Geldermalsen* was discovered by Englishman Mike Hatcher, a salvor who had spent years salvaging scrap metal and cargo from World War II wrecks, and his Swiss partner, Max de Rham. Hatcher began his search for the *Geldermalsen* in the early 1980s. At first, he found a 17th-century Chinese junk and salvaged its cargo of 25,000 pieces of porcelain. Then, in February 1985, his sidescan sonar located something on the seabed, at a depth of

passengers, including a seal with the initials "F.B." on it. It had belonged to Frederick Beckenhouwer, a surgeon known to have sailed on the *Geldermalsen*, and it was this object that helped to positively identify the ship.

TEA MADE UP THE BULK OF THE *GELDERMALSEN'S* CARGO

40 m (130 ft). Two divers went to investigate, and they found a ship's anchor, cannons, pieces of porcelain, and the ghostly outline of a wooden hull. During May and June, Hatcher raised 170,000 pieces of porcelain, 126 gold bars, the ship's bell, and personal objects that belonged to the crew and

Sale of the century

In salvaging the *Geldermalsen's* cargo, Hatcher acted as a treasure-hunter, out for personal gain. There were no attempts made to record the location of the artefacts, as an archaeologist would do. Valuable historical information was lost in the rush to raise the cargo. Hatcher was criticized by universities and museums, and even today there are still problems for him, since the government of the Netherlands claims it owns all wrecks of the Dutch East India Company. Also, the government of Indonesia claims it owns the wreck and its cargo, since the ship sank within her territorial

LOG ON...
Find out more:
www.vocshipwrecks.nl

waters, off the island of Bintan. Despite objections, the porcelain from the "Nanking Cargo Wreck" was sold by Christie's, at their salerooms in Amsterdam, Netherlands. Over five days in April and May, 1986, bidders paid high prices to own pieces of history. The national museum of the Netherlands (the Rijksmuseum) refused to have anything to do with the auction. The sale raised £10 million ($15 million), and the *Geldermalsen*'s cargo is now scattered between private and public

THE COVER OF CHRISTIE'S SALE CATALOGUE SHOWS PIECES OF THE CARGO.

THIS PLATE WAS AMONG THE THOUSANDS OF PIECES OF PORCELAIN SOLD AT THE AUCTION.

CHRISTIE'S
AMSTERDAM

collections all over the world. Antiques dealers are still selling pieces to collectors. But it wasn't all sold, since the sea didn't give up everything to the treasure-hunters – an estimated 32,500 cups and saucers, and 21 gold bars, are still on board the *Geldermalsen*.

WRECKED WARSHIPS

Warships have ruled the waves for thousands of years. The world's navies have sent awesome vessels into battle, from the ships of ancient Greece and Rome that destroyed their enemies with battering rams to the missile-firing battleships of the modern age. It's often the losing ships that we know most about, as they're the ones that became wrecks.

THE ANCIENT GREEKS USED THE NAVAL TACTIC OF RAMMING TO DEFEAT THE PERSIANS.

WEIRD WORLD

A FAVOURITE FIGHTING TACTIC OF THE ROMANS WAS TO MAKE A HIGH-SPEED PASS DOWN THE SIDE OF AN ENEMY WARSHIP, BREAKING OFF ITS OARS.

Weapon of destruction

In 1980, a 2.25 m- (7ft 4in-) long, wedge-shaped bronze object was pulled from the sea near the town of Athlit, Israel. Now called the "Athlit Ram", it revealed what the attacking end of an ancient Mediterranean warship looked like. The navies of ancient Greece and Rome fixed rams, like the Athlit Ram to the front of their rowing-ships at the water line. These armoured "beaks" were the main naval weapon of their day.

For some unknown reason, the Athlit Ram fell from its ship around 200 BC. Imagine how it might have seen action as oarsmen rowed their ship at speed until it collided with an enemy ship or a pirate vessel. As the ships met, the metal warhead was rammed home with force, cracking the enemy ship's timbers. When the damaged ship pulled away, the sea poured through the cracks in the hull, sending the ship to a watery grave.

An explosive powder

The discovery of an explosive black powder by Chinese scientists in about 850 AD brought the days of close-range fighting to an end. We call this powder "gunpowder". At first it was used by the Chinese to launch rockets in land battles. By the 1200s it was being used at sea for the long-range firing of projectiles from metal tubes, called cannons. Armies in Europe were using cannons by the 1300s, and they were soon fitted to the warships of the day. These were high-sided, timber vessels known as "cogs".

The first warships to fire cannons in anger fought in the Battle of Sluys (off the coast of present-day Netherlands) in

LOG ON...
www.maryrose.org/
explore/index.htm

COGS WERE STOCKY, STURDY SHIPS WITH A SINGLE MAST AND A SQUARE SAIL. THEY ALSO HAD A DEEP HULL.

1340, when English cogs destroyed a French fleet.

The *Mary Rose*

It isn't only enemy ships that cannons have sunk – sometimes they've played a part in sinking ships from their own side, as happened with the *Mary Rose*. On the morning of 19 July, 1545, the pride of the English fleet was sent to the bottom of the Solent, a narrow stretch of sea between the Isle of Wight and Portsmouth, England. On board were 91 cannons, a crew of about 400 men, and as many as 300 soldiers.

The reasons for the sinking are not clear, but it seems the ship was top-heavy, unbalanced by the weight of guns and men. When the *Mary Rose* turned to fire a broadside at ships of the French fleet, a gust of wind may have caught her, causing her to keel over, the tilt being made worse by the weight of the cannons on her upper decks. Water poured in through open gunports, and she sank in minutes. King Henry VIII watched from the shore as his favourite ship disappeared below the surface. Fewer than 40 men survived.

Cannons were expensive weapons, and over the next few years several were recovered so they could be reused. Then the wreck was forgotten. In 1836 it was rediscovered, and salvage work was carried out by a salvor called John Deane. He succeeded in raising several cannons, which were sold at auction. After this, the wreck was again forgotten. Finally, in 1965, archaeologists, led by Alexander McKee, started to look for the *Mary Rose*. She was

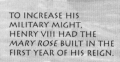

TO INCREASE HIS MILITARY MIGHT, HENRY VIII HAD THE *MARY ROSE* BUILT IN THE FIRST YEAR OF HIS REIGN.

ALL PARTS OF THE FRAGILE HULL WERE SUPPORTED EQUALLY SO THE *MARY ROSE* COULD BE LIFTED WITHOUT BEING DAMAGED.

found in 1971, buried beneath a deep layer of silt. Over the next 11 years an underwater excavation was carried out, led by Margaret Rule. Hoses sucked the mud away to reveal the skeletal remains of Henry VIII's flagship. More than 25,000 objects were mapped and lifted, including hundreds of Tudor weapons – cannons, longbows, arrows, swords, daggers, pikes, and fire darts. The remains of

brought to the surface, cradled inside a steel lifting frame. A large part of the wooden ship had survived its 437 years under water, but it was in a fragile state. It was brought ashore at Portsmouth and for 12 years the timbers were sprayed with fresh water to prevent them from drying out. The hull is now being sprayed

THE *MARY ROSE* WAS NAMED AFTER HENRY'S FAVOURITE SISTER

many soldiers and sailors were also discovered, a reminder that a warship wreck is often a grave.

Raising the *Rose*
On 11 October, 1982, millions of TV-viewers watched as the *Mary Rose* was

with a mixture of water and a type of wax (polyethylene glycol, or PEG), which makes old wood stronger.

THESE ENGLISH TUDOR COINS WERE RECOVERED FROM THE WRECK OF HENRY VIII'S FLAGSHIP, THE *MARY ROSE*.

DRIFTING FIRE SHIPS FORCED THE SPANISH ARMADA TO BREAK FORMATION. LONE SHIPS WERE THEN LEFT WITHOUT SUPPORT.

Spanish ships were anchored off Calais, France, the English sent fire ships (vessels deliberately set ablaze) towards them, forcing them to head north and sail around Britain and Ireland as they attempted to return home to Spain. It was a difficult journey, made worse by storms that blew many ships onto the islands' rocky coastlines. Only 60 ships made it back to Spain.

Many wrecks of the Spanish Armada have been discovered. Some have been excavated by archaeologists, who have uncovered a wealth of military objects, as well as the everyday possessions of an estimated 11,000 Spanish sailors who died when their ships were lost.

Eventually the sprays will be turned off, and the wood will be allowed to dry. The objects found on board the *Mary Rose* have also been carefully treated to preserve them for the future.

The Spanish Armada

The *Mary Rose* was not the only ship to sink off the coast of Britain in the 1500s. In July 1588, there was an attempt by Spain to invade England. A fleet, or armada, of 130 Spanish galleons, and other ships converted into warships, entered the English Channel. Between them they carried 2,500 cannons, and about 20,000 soldiers.

The Armada was met by 170 ships of the English fleet. The English plan was to prevent the Spaniards from putting their soldiers ashore. For a week the English shadowed the Armada, picking off ships that had drifted away from the main fleet. On 6 August, while the

Ghost ships

At the bottom of Lake Ontario, one of the Great Lakes of

WEIRD WORLD

DIVERS FOUND EIGHT GOLD CHAINS ON THE *GIRONA*, ONE OF THE WRECKED SHIPS OF THE ARMADA. THEY WERE A PRACTICAL KIND OF JEWELLERY, AS THE LINKS WERE UNSOLDERED SO THEY COULD BE DETACHED AND USED AS MONEY.

North America, lie two warships. Their names are *Hamilton* and *Scourge*. Although they ended their days as fighting ships, they began life carrying cargo around the lake.

transformed into the battleship *Hamilton*, and the *Lord Nelson* (a captured British trader) became the *Scourge*. Unfortunately for each ship, the heavy cannons taken on board (10 on the

MOST OF THE ARMADA'S LOST SHIPS WERE WRECKED BY STORMS ON THE COAST OF IRELAND, AND NOT BY ENGLISH VICTORIES.

In 1812 Britain and the USA went to war against each other, in a conflict that came to be known as the War of 1812. The American Navy had few ships, so ordinary merchant ships were hastily fitted out with cannons.
This was when the merchant ship *Diana* was

Hamilton, 8 on the *Scourge*) shifted their ship's centre of gravity, and each became unstable, just like the *Mary Rose*. On 8 August, 1813, a storm blew across the lake, and the vessels heeled over, capsized, and sank, taking 53 men with them. Eight survived.

Time passed until, in 1973, modern technology was used to locate the

RECOVERED FROM ONE OF THE ARMADA WRECKS, THIS PENDANT WAS BELIEVED TO PROTECT ITS WEARER FROM DEATH BY FIRE.

wrecks. What the searchers discovered was truly amazing. Far from being rotten, the ships were remarkably preserved. The cold water at the lake bottom, free of timber-eating organisms, had protected them.

Today, cannons are still in place on their gun carriages, and masts rise up from the decks, on which lie swords and boarding pikes. Nearby are the bones of dead sailors. One man's remains are tangled up in the *Scourge*'s rigging. The ships are like ghosts, strangely intact in the eerie darkness.

Sunk three times

It's a fact that wars result in the development of new types of ships and weapons. During the American Civil War (1861–65) two developments changed the course of war at sea. The first was the use of "ironclads" – steam-powered ships built of iron. They signalled the end of wooden warships, driven by wind and sail, and the arrival of battleships. The most famous ironclad was the USS *Monitor*, a vessel that was so low in the water it looked like a raft, on top of which was a revolving gun turret. She sank in high seas in 1862. Her wreck was located in 1973, and it is hoped that parts of this historic vessel can be raised.

The second warship development of America's civil

THE FIRST BATTLE BETWEEN IRONCLADS WAS IN 1862

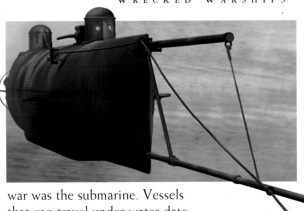

PACKED WITH EXPLOSIVE POWDER, THE *HUNLEY'S* TORPEDO WAS FITTED TO THE END OF A LONG HARPOON-LIKE ROD.

METAL ROD

TORPEDO

war was the submarine. Vessels that can travel under water date back to the 1600s, but this was the first war in which a submarine sank an enemy ship. The submarine was the CSS *H. L. Hunley*, named after its designer and captain, Horace L. Hunley. Built in 1863, the 12 m- (40 ft-) long iron cylinder was a true submersible, able to dive and surface. She was a hand-powered vessel with a crew of nine men – eight to turn the crank handle that spun her propeller, one to steer her. Her short life was beset by tragedy.

Before the *Hunley* had engaged her first enemy ship, she had sunk twice while being prepared for action. The first

time five of her crew died, the second time all nine drowned. After each sinking she was raised and made ready again. On 17 February, 1864, the *Hunley* sank for a third time – and this time she stayed down. It was also her moment of glory, the day she attacked the USS *Housatonic* as the enemy warship lay at anchor off Charleston, South Carolina. At the front of the submarine was a metal rod, about 7.6 m (25 ft) long. Attached to the end of it

THE *MONITOR* AND THE CONFEDERATE SHIP, *MERRIMACK* BATTLING DURING THE AMERICAN CIVIL WAR

was a torpedo packed with about 45 kg (100 lb) of gunpowder. The plan was to ram the *Housatonic* with the barbed tip of the rod, attach the torpedo to the ship's hull, then detonate it by pulling a cord from a safe distance. But something went wrong, and although the torpedo sank the *Housatonic*, the *Hunley* sank, too, taking her brave sub-mariners with her. Perhaps she was too close to the *Housatonic* when the torpedo exploded, and the shockwave from the blast destroyed both vessels. In 1995, The *Hunley* was found in 10 m (33 ft) of water.

She was raised in 2000, and is now being conserved and made ready for display.

Recent wrecks

A warship that can never be raised is the German battleship *Bismarck*, sunk in 1940 during World War II (1939–45). She lies in 4,600 m (15,000 ft) of water, on the floor of the North Atlantic Ocean, visited occasionally by a submersible whose mission is to video her.

The *Bismarck* was one of

PHOTOGRAPHED FROM HMS *PRINCE OF WALES*, THIS PICTURE OF HMS *HOOD* WAS TAKEN BEFORE SHE WENT INTO ACTION AGAINST THE BATTLESHIP *BISMARCK*.

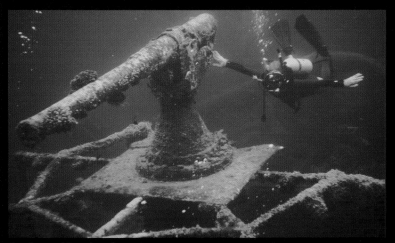

the last of her kind, and as warship design changed, the days of big-gunned battleships ended. In their place came aircraft carriers and submarines. Navies soon had to endure attacks from the sky, too.

ANTI-AIRCRAFT GUNS AND TANK TURRETS ON THE SEABED OF TRUK LAGOON ARE CLOAKED BY PLUMES OF SOFT CORAL.

Caught by surprise
During World War II, Japan and the USA each launched a surprise air attack on one another. The navies of both sides suffered massive losses. The first attack was in 1941, when Japanese aircraft struck a US Pacific Fleet, moored at Pearl Harbor on the Hawaiian island of Oahu. Within a mere two hours, five battleships had been sunk, another 16 damaged, and 188

aircraft destroyed. In February 1944, the USA began "Operation Hailstorm", and dealt a devastating blow to the Japanese Imperial fleet, sinking over 45 ships, including armed cargo ships, huge tankers, small destroyers and a submarine. More than 416 planes were also sent to their final resting place, the tranquil ocean floor of Truk Lagoon, in the Pacific Ocean. Almost 60 years later, these relics of war can be found on magnificent coral reefs, housing countless tropical fish and anemones.

WEIRD WORLD
THE RUSSIAN NUCLEAR-POWERED SUBMARINE *KURSK* WAS SUNK BY ITS OWN TORPEDO IN 2000. A FAULT IN THE WEAPON HAD CAUSED IT TO EXPLODE IN THE TORPEDO ROOM, AND THE BLAST BLEW A HOLE IN THE PRESSURIZED HULL.

RAISING THE VASA

When a warship fires its guns, their deafening noise rolls out over the waves like peals of thunder. But for one warship this was not to be. Her 64 great guns were never fired in anger, for they slipped silently below the waves the day the man-of-war left Stockholm harbour, Sweden. The year was 1628. The ship was the *Vasa*, and she sank on her maiden voyage.

Sweden's sea power
Starting in the early 1600s, Sweden took control of land beyond her own borders, in countries that form today Norway, Finland, Germany, Poland, Latvia, Estonia, Lithuania, and Russia. For Sweden to maintain her growing empire, and defend it from hostile nations, it was vital for her to become the supreme sea power of the region. This meant controlling the Baltic Sea – the sea that bordered her territories. In 1620, Sweden's king, Gustav II Adolf ordered 25 new

warships to be built to increase the size and strength of his navy. But more ships were needed, and in 1626 the king ordered another one to be built – the *Vasa*. It was named after his grandfather, King Gustav I Vasa.

Building the *Vasa*

The king's newest ship was also his grandest. She was built in a Stockholm shipyard by a Dutch master shipbuilder, Henrik Hybertsson, who had built many ships for the Swedish navy. He mainly used Swedish oak, and built the *Vasa* according to a design he carried in his head (shipbuilders of the day liked to keep their knowledge a secret). The ship was 62 m (204 ft) long, 11.7 m (39 ft) wide, 20 m (65 ft) high at the stern (back), and the tip of her mainmast was 50 m (165 ft) above her keel (the timber along the bottom of the hull). She was a heavily armed gunship, equipped with bronze cannons that could shoot cannonballs over distances of up to 1,500 m (5,000 ft). Her guns added an extra 72 tonnes to her weight.

LOG ON...
www.vasamuseet.se/
indexeng.html

WEIRD WORLD
IN THE 1920S, A MAGICIAN SEARCHED FOR THE *VASA* WITH A DIVINING ROD MADE OF SOLID GOLD. HE FOUND NOTHING.

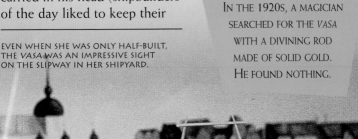

EVEN WHEN SHE WAS ONLY HALF-BUILT, THE *VASA* WAS AN IMPRESSIVE SIGHT ON THE SLIPWAY IN HER SHIPYARD.

THE SWEDISH SALVORS, WHO RECOVERED THE *VASA'S* CANNONS, HAD TO WORK IN PITCH BLACKNESS WHILE INSIDE THEIR PRIMITIVE DIVING BELL.

Day of disaster

By early August 1628, the *Vasa* was ready for her maiden voyage. She was to join other ships of the Swedish fleet patrolling the Baltic coasts of Poland and Germany. On 10 August, crowds waved as she sailed from Stockholm quayside. No one knows how many people were on board, but it was probably around 150 on board lost their lives. An inquiry was held, and although no one was blamed, all agreed the ship was poorly designed. Like the *Mary Rose* before her, and the *Hamilton* and *Scourge* after her, the *Vasa* was top-heavy with guns, and there was not enough ballast in the hold to keep her stable. When the wind blew, she was unbalanced, and over she went.

THE *VASA* DID NOT HAVE A FULL CREW ON HER MAIDEN VOYAGE

men and women (some of the crewmen's wives went, too). It was to be a very short voyage.

After travelling only 1,400 m (4,500 ft), the *Vasa's* sails filled with a sudden gust of wind and she heeled over. Her captain, Sofring Hansson, had sailed with the ship's gunports open, so water rushed in. The *Vasa* flooded, and she sank in 35 m (115 ft) of water. Only the tops of her masts were left poking above the water.

Sweden had lost her finest warship and about 50 of those

Salvage operations

Within days of the disaster attempts were made at salvaging the *Vasa's* valuable cannons. An English salvor, Ian Bulmer, tried first, followed by the Swedish Navy. Both failed. It was not until 1664 that a team of Swedish salvors, working from inside a primitive diving bell, was successful. They raised 53 of the *Vasa's* 64 cannons, each weighing 1–2 tonnes. It was quite a feat for the time. With most of the guns recovered, the *Vasa* was abandoned. As her masts rotted and fell, she faded to all but a distant memory. Only in the 20th century was interest in her revived, and in 1956, historian Anders Franzén located Sweden's famous lost warship.

ONCE SHE HAD SURFACED, THE *VASA'S* HULL WAS WAS MADE WATERTIGHT. THE GREAT WARSHIP WAS THEN ABLE TO FLOAT.

THE *VASA* UNDERWENT A LONG PROCESS OF TREATMENT TO CONSERVE HER TIMBERS AND STOP THEM FROM DECAYING.

Raised and saved

The Swedish government decided to raise the *Vasa*. Nothing like this had ever been attempted for such a big vessel. It took five years of preparation work, and a total of 1,300 dives by Swedish Navy divers, before the *Vasa* could be brought to the surface. On 24 April, 1961, the lifting barges *Odin* and *Frigg* took the strain and the *Vasa* emerged into the daylight for the first time in 333 years. Then the long and difficult job of saving her timbers from drying out began. For 17 years the hull was sprayed with a waxy substance, called polyethylene glycol (PEG),

ornaments. They included the Swedish coat-of-arms, chubby angels, and figures of warriors in suits of armour. Sculpted from oak, pine, and lime woods, these beautiful objects were among the retrieved items.

which soaked into the timbers and drove out the salty water. Only when the timbers had absorbed as much PEG as possible, were they allowed to slowly dry, without fear of them cracking.

Today, the *Vasa* has been restored to her former glory, and she is on display in a purpose-built museum in Stockholm. She is the only warship from the 1600s to be seen anywhere in the world.

Bones, boots, and butter

It wasn't just the *Vasa's* hull that was pulled from the deep. Some 15,000 objects were also recovered, from seamen's chests packed with everyday personal objects, such as leather boots and felt hats, to six huge sails, which were stored in the *Vasa's* sail locker. Even a tub of butter was found! The bones of 25 people were discovered, too. These unlucky mariners were given a proper burial in 1963.

The *Vasa* is more than a warship – she is also an art treasure. To give her a lavish appearance, skilled woodcarvers from Germany and the Netherlands decorated her with more than 700 figures and

OTHE CARVINGS ON THE STERN REVEAL THE SKILLS OF THE WOODCARVERS.

THE *VASA* IS SHOWN BELOW ON DISPLAY IN ITS MUSEUM IN STOCKHOLM.

PLUNDERING PIRATES

It's lonely at sea, and sailors can travel a long time without sighting land or other vessels. Imagine if, from out of the blue, they spy a ship approaching them, their first contact in days or weeks with fellow seafarers. As the ship nears, its purpose becomes clear – to attack and raid its victim, stealing its cargo and even the ship itself. This is the age-old problem of piracy.

Ancient pirates

Pirates have plagued the ocean since ancient times. As if proof was needed, the wreck of a 2,300-year-old Greek merchant ship, found on the seabed off the coast of Cyprus in the 1960s, showed

MANY FILMS HAVE BEEN MADE ABOUT THE LIVES AND EXPLOITS OF PIRATES. THIS IS A SCENE FROM *PIRATES*, A FILM MADE IN 1986.

tell-tale signs of having been attacked. Now known as the Kyrenia Ship, after the nearby town of that name, eight iron spearpoints were found stabbed into its hull. This is evidence, say the archaeologists who excavated the site, of a pirate raid. If this ship was a victim of pirates, they would have stripped it of its valuables, and probably sold its crew into slavery, as they would have been little more than cargo that could be sold for profit. By sinking the ship, all evidence of their crime was sent to the bottom of the sea.

WEIRD WORLD

IN 76 BC, THE GREAT ROMAN STATESMAN, JULIUS CAESAR, WAS CAPTURED IN THE MEDITERRANEAN SEA BY PIRATES. HE WAS RELEASED AFTER A SUM OF MONEY HAD BEEN GIVEN TO THEM.

Mediterranean pirates

The Romans were also pestered by pirates, though they eventually got the better of them. In 67 BC, Pompey (106–48 BC), a

THIS 20TH-CENTURY PAINTING SHOWS PIRATES IN THE 1600S. THEY ARE USING A SMALL VESSEL TO SNEAK UP ON THEIR PRIZE – AN UNFORTUNATE GALLEON.

pirates are known), captured 98 warships and hundreds of smaller craft, and saw their ill-gotten gains shipped away to Rome. It was a setback that lasted as long as the Roman Empire, but with its collapse in the AD 400s, the pirates returned, and the seas around Europe were once more lawless places in which to sail.

The Golden Age

The so-called "Golden Age" of piracy, a period of little more than 40 years between about 1690 and 1730, is the time that most people think of at the mention of the word "pirate". Many of these outlaws worked among the islands of the Caribbean Sea, and as many as 2,000 sea-wolves were said to operate here in the early 1700s. Some are famous – or infamous – for their acts of daring and brutality. Among them was Edward Teach, known as "Blackbeard", who terrorized the North American coast. There was also Edward Low, of whom it was said, "a greater monster never infested the seas". John Rackham, known as

ruthless military general, headed a major land and sea campaign to rid the Roman world of pirates from Cilicia, a pirate haven along the present-day coast of Turkey. With a taskforce of some 270 ships, 120,000 soldiers, and 5,000 cavalry, Pompey crushed the pirates in a three-month campaign that killed 10,000 of the corsairs (as Mediterranean

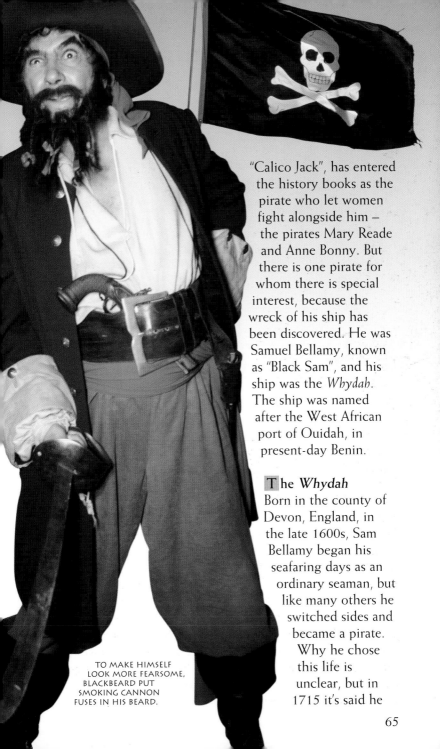

"Calico Jack", has entered the history books as the pirate who let women fight alongside him – the pirates Mary Reade and Anne Bonny. But there is one pirate for whom there is special interest, because the wreck of his ship has been discovered. He was Samuel Bellamy, known as "Black Sam", and his ship was the *Whydah*. The ship was named after the West African port of Ouidah, in present-day Benin.

The *Whydah*

Born in the county of Devon, England, in the late 1600s, Sam Bellamy began his seafaring days as an ordinary seaman, but like many others he switched sides and became a pirate. Why he chose this life is unclear, but in 1715 it's said he

TO MAKE HIMSELF LOOK MORE FEARSOME, BLACKBEARD PUT SMOKING CANNON FUSES IN HIS BEARD.

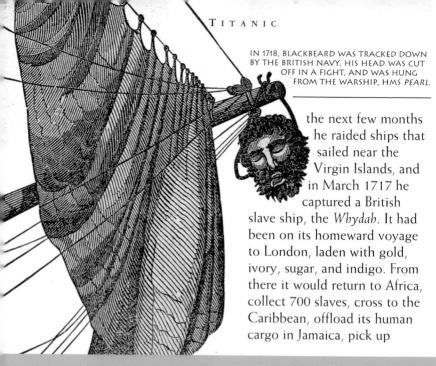

IN 1718, BLACKBEARD WAS TRACKED DOWN BY THE BRITISH NAVY. HIS HEAD WAS CUT OFF IN A FIGHT, AND WAS HUNG FROM THE WARSHIP, HMS *PEARL*.

the next few months he raided ships that sailed near the Virgin Islands, and in March 1717 he captured a British slave ship, the *Whydah*. It had been on its homeward voyage to London, laden with gold, ivory, sugar, and indigo. From there it would return to Africa, collect 700 slaves, cross to the Caribbean, offload its human cargo in Jamaica, pick up

A PIRATE'S LEG WAS RETRIEVED FROM THE *WHYDAH'S* WRECK SITE

was working on the salvage of a Spanish treasure ship, off the coast of Florida, USA. Following an argument with his employers, perhaps over how the salvage was to be shared out, he turned against them and raided their campsite.

In 1716 Bellamy sailed with the pirate Benjamin Hornigold (Edward Teach was another of his crew). By August that year Bellamy had fallen out with Hornigold and had decided to work alone, commanding his own ship, the *Mary Anne*. For

goods, then sail home to Britain. There were hundreds of other ships involved in this "triangular trade", but the *Whydah* was the one that fell prey to Sam Bellamy.

The *Whydah* became Bellamy's flagship, and he armed her with 28 cannons. In the weeks that followed her conversion from slaver to raider, Bellamy sailed her along the Atlantic coast of North America, robbing ships as he went. Then disaster struck. During the night of 17 May,

DIVERS SURFACE FROM THE *WHYDAH* WRECK SITE WITH A HAUL OF SPANISH SILVER COINS KNOW AS "PIECES OF EIGHT".

LOG ON...
www.whydah.com/
page.php?id=exp0

1717, the *Whydah* foundered on a sandbank and broke in two, close to Cape Cod, Massachusetts, USA. Bellamy and 143 of his crew drowned. Only two men survived, and they were arrested as they scrambled ashore.

Discovery of the *Whydah*

With a wrecked pirate ship lying close to shore, attempts were quickly made to salvage her looted treasure – thousands of gold and silver coins, said to weigh 4.5 tonnes. It had been plundered from more than 50 vessels, but little was recovered, and the sea and sand slowly covered the ship's remains. Only in 1984 did the sea start to give up the treasure of the *Whydah*, to Barry Clifford, an American treasure hunter. Clifford has found more than 100,000 objects scattered on the seabed, from coins and cannons to leather boots and musket balls – the first artefacts ever recovered from an authentic pirate shipwreck.

There was no doubt that after 15 years of searching Clifford had found Bellamy's treasure ship, for in 1985 he raised the ship's bell, on which were the words "The Whydah Gally 1716". But one thing still eludes him – the ship's mother lode of treasure, which one of the two survivors said amounted to 180 bags of gold and silver. The search continues, and Barry Clifford knows that what he discovers will be his, because the State of Massachusetts lets finders be keepers.

PIRATE LOOT – GOLD AND SILVER COINS, AND A FINGER RING, RECOVERED FROM THE WRECK OF THE *WHYDAH*.

LOST LINERS

Ask anyone to name the world's most famous lost liner, and they will probably say the *Titanic*. They'd be right, of course, but try asking them to name another liner, and they might not be so quick with their reply. The sad fact is, the *Titanic* is just one of many great passenger ships that have ended their days on the seabed. These ships are the subject of endless fascination, speculation, and mystery, and they all have stories to tell.

Sailing the line

Look in most old atlases (and some modern ones) and you'll see dotted lines marked across the world's oceans. At the end of each line is a destination, a port. The line itself shows the route a passenger ship takes as it crosses the sea from country to country. It is because the ship follows this fixed line that it is known as a "liner".

There are fewer liners crossing the seas today, because travel by air is both cheaper and faster. Instead of liners, today's people-movers are luxury cruise ships – pleasure boats on which passengers can enjoy a special holiday.

In 1970 cruise ships carried 0.5 million people, by 2000 it was 7 million. These ships are getting bigger and carrying more people, but the age of ocean-going liners is not completely over. In 2004 the *Queen Mary II* will sail from Southampton, England, to New York, USA, on her maiden voyage. On board will be up to 3,850 passengers and crew, sailing a similar

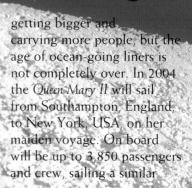

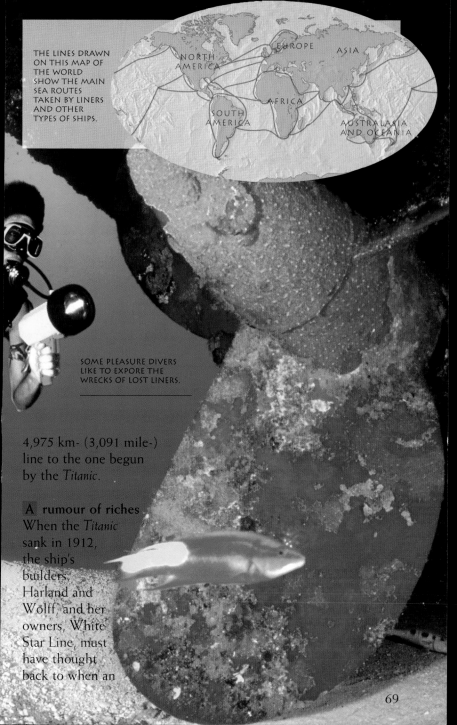

THE LINES DRAWN
ON THIS MAP OF
THE WORLD
SHOW THE MAIN
SEA ROUTES
TAKEN BY LINERS
AND OTHER
TYPES OF SHIPS.

NORTH
AMERICA

EUROPE

ASIA

AFRICA

SOUTH
AMERICA

AUSTRALASIA
AND OCEANIA

SOME PLEASURE DIVERS
LIKE TO EXPORE THE
WRECKS OF LOST LINERS.

4,975 km- (3,091 mile-)
line to the one begun
by the *Titanic*.

A rumour of riches
When the *Titanic*
sank in 1912,
the ship's
builders,
Harland and
Wolff, and her
owners, White
Star Line, must
have thought
back to when an

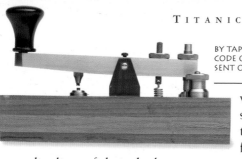

BY TAPPING OUT THE ALPHABET IN MORSE CODE ON A TELEGRAPH KEY, OPERATORS SENT OUT MESSAGES LETTER BY LETTER.

earlier liner of theirs had perished. It was as if history was repeating itself. The ship was the *Republic*. It was launched in 1903. Half the size of the *Titanic*, the *Republic* steamed out of New York wireless distress signal ever sent from a sinking ship, the forerunner of the more famous SOS signal. All passengers and most of the crew were ferried by lifeboat to the *Florida*. The few crew who remained were later rescued by another ship. Although an attempt was made to tow the stricken *Republic* to safety, it

THE *REPUBLIC* WAS BUILT IN THE SAME SHIPYARD AS THE *TITANIC*

harbour on January 22, 1909, bound for Italy. On board were about 750 passengers and crew.

Not far out of New York, the *Republic* sailed into thick fog, and collided with an Italian liner, the *Florida*. As water flooded the *Republic*'s engine room and the ship began to list, the wireless operator tapped out in Morse Code the international distress signal, CQD (CQ for "All Stations, Attention", and D for "Distress"). It was the first

WHETHER OR NOT THERE REALLY ARE GOLD COINS TO BE FOUND IS THE LASTING MYSTERY – OR MYTH – OF THE *REPUBLIC*.

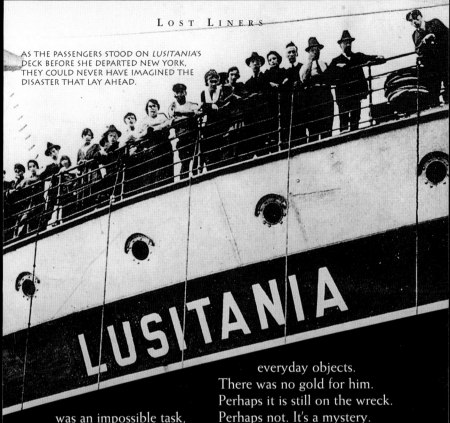

AS THE PASSENGERS STOOD ON *LUSITANIA*'S DECK BEFORE SHE DEPARTED NEW YORK, THEY COULD NEVER HAVE IMAGINED THE DISASTER THAT LAY AHEAD.

LUSITANIA

was an impossible task, and she sank in 80 m (260 ft) of water. A rumour soon spread that a fortune in American gold coins was also lost.

Rumours about treasure niggle away inside the minds of salvors and treasure-hunters, and although no one knew for certain if the *Republic* did have a stash of cash, Martin Bayerle, an American wreck hunter, wanted to find out. In 1981 he located the *Republic*, and in 1987 his salvage company began the first exploration of the site, finding only wine bottles, dinner plates, and other everyday objects. There was no gold for him. Perhaps it is still on the wreck. Perhaps not. It's a mystery.

Casualty of war

In the early years of the 20th century it must have seemed that fate had conspired to sink a great liner every three years: the *Republic* in 1909, the *Titanic* in 1912, and the *Lusitania* in 1915. While the first two were victims of bad weather and bad design, the *Lusitania* was an unfortunate victim of World War I (1914–18).

Launched in 1907, the *Lusitania* was a luxury liner, built to ferry passengers from Britain to America. She was the first

A SECTION WAS BLASTED AWAY FROM THE *LUSITANIA'S* HULL, AND HER FORWARD MOMENTUM ACCELERATED THE FLOODING.

ship to make the crossing in less than five days.

On 1 May, 1915, she steamed away from New York, bound for Liverpool, England, at the start of her 202nd trans-Atlantic crossing. There were 1,257 passengers and 702 crew on board. That same day, the German government announced that any ship entering the war zone around Britain (Britain and Germany had been at war since August 1914) would be attacked.

During the afternoon of 7 May, 1915, as the *Lusitania* passed the coast of Ireland, she

THE *LUSITANIA* SANK SO QUICKLY, THERE WAS BARELY ANY TIME FOR HER PASSENGERS AND CREW TO ESCAPE.

was torpedoed by the German submarine U–20. Her boilers exploded, she listed dangerously, and just 18 minutes after the attack the 30,396-tonne ship sank in 90 m (300 ft) of water, taking 1,198 people to their graves. It was an outrage that stunned Britain and America, and brought the USA into the war against Germany. It also sparked a flurry of rumours that claimed the *Lusitania* had been carrying supplies of arms, as well as a fortune in gold bullion and diamonds, and a collection of priceless paintings.

The truth is out there

Had the *Lusitania* been carrying weapons? Did she really have a fortune in gold and gems? Since the first salvage attempts in the 1930s, these were the questions that many asked, but only in the 1980s did the truth start to come out, as the first real work was done on exploring the ship. Rifle cartridges and fuses for explosive shells were found, proving the liner had

THIS OLD ILLUSTRATION SHOWS DIVERS RAISING THE *EGYPT*'S CARGO. IN REALITY, A GRAB WAS FOUND TO BE MORE EFFECTIVE.

been shipping arms from America to Britain. As for the treasure, nothing has ever been discovered. Perhaps that was a rumour after all, or perhaps it has yet to be found.

Egypt's two treasures

By a strange twist of fate, a liner carrying gold and silver bullion that sank in 1922 was called the *Egypt*. Later that same year the fabulous treasure of the ancient Egyptian boy-pharaoh Tutankhamun was discovered in Egypt's Valley of the Kings. While one treasure of Egypt was found, another was lost.

Unlike the *Lusitania*, there is no doubt about the valuable cargo that was stored in the *Egypt*'s hold. On 19 May, 1922, she departed London, bound for Bombay (modern Mumbai),

India. As she was rounding the tip of Brittany, France, she ran into thick fog, and then another ship, the *Seine*, ploughed into her. Within 20 minutes the *Egypt* had sunk, with the loss of 86 of the 342 people on board. Her cargo of 1,089 bars of gold, 1,229 bars of silver, and 164,979 gold sovereigns (British coins) went to the Atlantic seabed.

In deep water

The *Egypt* sank in 120 m (400 ft) of water – a depth which, in 1922, was deeper than a diver could reach. This didn't stop salvors from searching for the wreck. They used a long cable stretched between two ships. It was dragged along the seabed until it snagged on a submerged object. This was the method used to find the *Egypt* in 1930. By then the technology existed to lower a man to the wreck inside a steel observation chamber. Albert Gianni, an Italian diver, was the man chosen for this job. He spoke to the men on the salvage ship by telephone, instructing them where to lower explosives onto the wreck. After using five tonnes of TNT explosives to rip through the ship's steel decks, the strongroom was reached, and a grab was lowered to haul out its valuable contents.

In June 1932 some gold and a pile of ingots and coins were retrieved. Over the next three years 95 per cent of the *Egypt*'s treasure was recovered. Today, all that's left on the *Egypt* are 17 gold bars, 30 silver bars, and 14,929 gold sovereigns.

LOG ON...
More than 40 lost liners:
www.lostliners.com

THIS PHOTOGRAPH SHOWS THE TRIUMPHANT SALVORS WITH SOME OF THE *EGYPT*'S GOLD.

SURVIVORS' STORIES

A sinking ship can bring out the best – and the worst – in human nature. Survivors have told tales of incredible acts of bravery and heroism, as well as accounts of how desperate people have resorted to desperate measures. Every shipwreck survivor is a life saved, but it can also mean a person's life changed forever, especially if they have survived against the odds.

Moby Dick, the true story
In the 19th century, an American author called Herman Melville used the true story of a shipwrecked whaler, Owen Chase, as the basis for his book *Moby Dick*. Also known as *The Whale*, his novel was published in 1851.

years. Few of them ever did because on 20 November, 1820, the *Essex* was attacked by a sperm whale, said to be 26 m (85 ft) long. The enormous whale head-butted the *Essex* twice, and in the second charge it punched a hole through the wooden hull.

THE *ESSEX* WAS STRUCK BY A WHALE AS LONG AS ITSELF

The facts of the real Moby Dick story are these. In August 1819, the whaling ship *Essex* left Nantucket, Massachusetts, USA, bound for the South Pacific, in search of sperm whales. It was to be a long voyage, and none of the 21 crew expected to see their home port again for three

Twenty men, one of them Owen Chase, scrambled into the ship's three small whaling boats with whatever food and fresh water they could grab. Within ten minutes of the whale's attack, the *Essex* had capsized, and the survivors were cast out into the vastness of the Atlantic Ocean.

Eating your shipmates

On December 20, after 31 days adrift, the 20 survivors landed on a small island, but there was little there for them to eat. Reluctantly, 17 men decided to take to the sea again in the three boats, hoping to reach South America. Three men stayed on the island. Five set sail in Owen Chase's boat, and after a further 24 days at sea, one of them died. He was buried at sea. Three weeks later, a second man, Isaac Cole, passed away. Rather than tip him over the side for fishfood, his corpse became food for Chase and his two companions, Ben Lawrence and Tom Nickerson. Forced to resort to cannibalism, the men lived off Cole's body for a week. Had they not done so, they wouldn't have lasted long enough to see the welcome sight of the ship, the *Indian* which rescued them on 18 February, 1821, after 90 days at sea.

IN 1956, HERMAN MELVILLE'S *MOBY DICK* WAS ADAPTED FOR THE SCREEN. THIS SCENE FROM THE FILM SHOWS THE ILL-EQUIPPED OWEN CHASE FACING HIS FOE – THE SPERM WHALE THAT HAD CAPSIZED HIS SHIP.

Of the other boats, the second was never seen again, while the men of the third became more than cannibals, and murdered two of their companions to satisfy their hunger. After 95 days at sea, the two survivors of this boat were picked up by a passing ship, the *Dauphin*. All of the men on the island survived.

WEIRD WORLD

IN 2001, THREE MEN STAYED ALIVE, AFTER THEIR SHIP SANK IN THE CARIBBEAN SEA, BY EATING THE BODIES OF FELLOW VOYAGERS WHO DIED DURING A THREE-WEEK ORDEAL AT SEA.

lifeboats for just four hours, until rescued by the liner *Carpathia*. It had responded to the *Titanic*'s SOS distress signal, and had steamed through the night to the *Titanic*'s position after receiving her plea for help: "Come at once. We have struck an iceberg." At dawn on April 15, 1912, the few *Titanic* survivors climbed up rope ladders and nets, or were hauled up in slings, onto the deck of the *Carpathia*.

Titanic survivors

Mercifully for the *Titanic* survivors, no one needed to resort to cannibalism to stay alive. Unlike the men of the *Essex*, who endured three months at sea, the 706 people who escaped from the great ship drifted in her

TITANIC'S SURVIVORS ROWED THEIR LIFEBOATS CLEAR OF THE SINKING SHIP TO AVOID BEING DRAGGED UNDERWATER.

HUDDLED TOGETHER ON THE DECK OF THE *CARPATHIA*, THE *TITANIC* SURVIVORS WERE OFFERED BLANKETS AND BRANDY.

Three days later, on Thursday, 18 April, the *Carpathia* arrived in New York, USA, the very destination the *Titanic* had been bound for. Only then did the true tragedy of the disaster come out, as the survivors told their stories. Some, such as Bruce Ismay, whose company owned the ship, were so affected by the disaster they couldn't speak of it. It was forbidden even to mention the ship's name to Ismay.

Heroine of the *Titanic*

Perhaps the most famous *Titanic* survivor was Margaret Brown. A woman of great character, she put the safety of others before her own as she helped survivors into the *Titanic*'s lifeboats, before finally saving herself. She could have left sooner, since women and children were instructed to leave the ship first, followed later by the men. On board the *Carpathia* she continued to help her fellow survivors, and by the time the rescue ship berthed in New York, Margaret Brown

had helped organize the Titanic Survivor's Committee. To her dying day (in 1932), Margaret Brown worked to preserve the memory of those who had died on the *Titanic*, and those who had survived.

Saved by a bucket

It's often a miracle that some people survive a shipwreck at all, especially if the ship has no lifeboats, life jackets, radios or other emergency equipment.

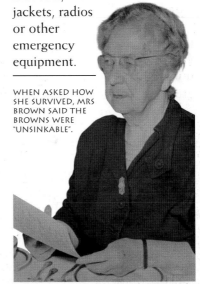

WHEN ASKED HOW SHE SURVIVED, MRS BROWN SAID THE BROWNS WERE "UNSINKABLE".

THE AUSTRALIAN NAVY FRIGATE, HMAS ADELAIDE SENT A CREW IN AN INFLATABLE TO RESCUE BULLIMORE FROM HIS YACHT.

You might think this describes a ship from long ago, but, tragically, it doesn't. The dangerously overcrowded ferry boat *Neptune* was one such ill-equipped ship. When it sank in a storm off the coast of Haiti, in the Caribbean Sea, in February 1993, all but 285 of its 2,000 passengers died (the ferry should not have carried more than 650 people).

Reports said that as the vessel had started to pitch and roll in the choppy seas, the people on board panicked and rushed to one side of the ship, causing it to capsize. As men, women, and children struggled for survival in the water, one man grabbed a bag of charcoal and clung to it for dear life. He was one of the lucky few who lived to tell his tale. Another survivor was a woman who held onto a plastic bucket until rescue boats arrived.

Alone at sea

The *Neptune* sank close to land, and none of the survivors spent longer than a few hours in the sea. Tony Bullimore's story is almost the exact opposite of theirs. In 1997, he took part in a single-handed, round-the-world race in his 18 m- (60 ft-) yacht *Exide Challenger*. As he crossed the Southern Ocean, 800 km (500 miles) north of the coast of Antarctica, his boat

Bullimore's upturned boat was spotted on day four by an Australian Air Force plane, but he was nowhere to be seen. Having run out of drinking water, and with little to eat, his situation

LOG ON...
www.bbc.co.uk/
dna/h2g2/A671492

BULLIMORE LIVED ON CHOCOLATE AND WATER DURING HIS ORDEAL

was hit by a severe storm. Over and over the boat rolled, finally coming to rest upside down – with Bullimore trapped in an air pocket inside. The world held its breath for five days as teams from the Australian rescue services headed to him.

was desperate, but on day five he heard banging on the hull of his yacht. Knowing he'd been found, Bullimore dived from under his yacht and surfaced alongside a rescue boat. His five-day ordeal was over.

ALTHOUGH HE WAS COLD, DEHYDRATED AND HUNGRY, BULLIMORE WAS FOUND TO BE IN REMARKABLY GOOD HEALTH.

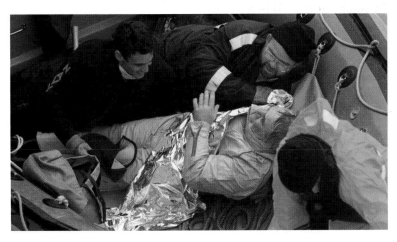

ALL WASHED UP!

Somewhere in the world today a ship was wrecked. The same thing happened yesterday, and it will happen again tomorrow. Whatever the type of ship, and no matter when or how it met with disaster, the effects of its loss reach more people than those unlucky enough to have sailed on her. A shipwreck affects the lives of people on land, too.

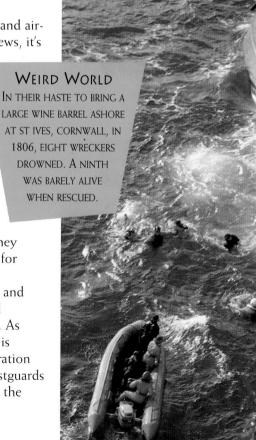

To the rescue

For the world's lifeboat and air-sea rescue helicopter crews, it's all in a day's work to pluck people to safety from a stricken ship. They also rescue people from life rafts, pieces of floating wreckage, or they may fish them out of the water itself. These brave rescuers work in all weathers, knowing they could be the only hope for mariners in distress.

Good communication and speed are essential to all successful rescue efforts. As soon as a distress signal is picked up, a rescue operation swings into action. Coastguards pinpoint the location of the vessel with the help of

WEIRD WORLD
IN THEIR HASTE TO BRING A LARGE WINE BARREL ASHORE AT ST IVES, CORNWALL, IN 1806, EIGHT WRECKERS DROWNED. A NINTH WAS BARELY ALIVE WHEN RESCUED.

A HELICOPTER CAN LIFT PEOPLE TO SAFETY, THEN SPEED THOSE WHO ARE INJURED TO HOSPITAL FOR TREATMENT.

satellites, then pass the information to the rescue services, who race to the scene of the accident as fast as they can.

But what happens if the vessel is so far from land that a lifeboat or helicopter can't reach it in time? In these cases, nearby ships will go to its aid, as happened when the *Carpathia* became the rescue ship for the survivors from the *Titanic*.

Washed ashore

People who live around the world's coastlines know only too well that the sea brings many surprises. They watch as their town's lifeboat is launched, or as a rescue aircraft flies overhead, wondering what ship has called it, and why, and hoping that the rescuers, and the people they've gone to rescue, return safely.

With each high tide a new "crop" of flotsam (floating wreckage) comes ashore. As it's washed onto the beaches, different groups of people become caught up in shipwreck stories.

LIFEBOATS RANGE FROM SMALL INSHORE INFLATABLES LIKE THE ONE IN THIS PICTURE, TO LARGE OFFSHORE VESSELS.

Environmental organizations have the messy task of cleaning spilled oil (and other chemicals) from rocks, sand, and animals when oil tankers lose their load. This happened in 1989 when the *Exxon Valdez* spilled 38,800 tonnes of crude oil into the Prince William Sound, Alaska, USA.

Shipwrecks can bring rich pickings, too, not just for salvors, treasure-hunters, and archaeologists, but for wreckers (people who take cargo that's washed ashore). The people of Cornwall, England, know all about wrecking. In February 2002, the *Kodima* ran aground in Whitsand Bay, on the south coast of Cornwall, during a force 8 gale. It shed a massive load of Swedish timber. Thousands of planks of wood were washed from its cargo hold onto the Cornish beaches. Although it was illegal to do so, people travelled from far and wide to gather the wood for themselves. One man took enough timber to make a shed.

Next time you find a piece of driftwood on a beach, ask yourself where it came from. Perhaps it was once part of a ship's cargo, perhaps it was part of the ship herself. You can be certain of one thing, that if it could speak, it would have quite a story to tell.

THE *KODIMA'S* LOST CARGO OF TIMBER COMPLETELY COVERED BEACHES ON THE SOUTH COAST OF CORNWALL.

REFERENCE SECTION

Whether you've finished reading *Titanic*, or are turning to this section first, you'll find the information on the next eight pages really useful. Here are all the shipwreck facts and figures, background details, and some unfamiliar nautical words that you might need. You'll also find a list of website addresses – so, whether you want to surf the net or search out facts, these pages should turn you from an enthusiast into an expert.

TITANIC TIMELINE

Summer, 1907
Bruce Ismay and Lord William Pirrie meet in London. Plans are made to build two luxury liners, named later as the *Olympic* and the *Titanic*, with a third, the *Gigantic*, to be built after them (it was renamed the *Britannic*).

31 March, 1909
Titanic's keel laid down at Harland and Wolff shipyard, Belfast, Ireland.

31 May, 1911
The hull of the *Titanic* is launched, watched by 100,000 people.

20 March, 1912
Original date planned for *Titanic's* departure on her maiden voyage. It was rescheduled for 10 April.

31 March
The outfitting of the *Titanic* is complete. She is ready to sail.

2 April
6.00 am: Sea trials begin. All equipment is tested.
8.00 pm: Leaves Belfast bound for Southampton, 917 km (570 miles) to the south.

3–4 April
Midnight: Arrives at Southampton, England.

10 April: Wednesday
9.30–11.30 pm: Passengers board.
12.15 pm: Departs Southampton.
6.30 pm: Departs Cherbourg, France.

11 April: Thursday
1.30 pm: Departs Queenstown, Ireland, with 2,223 people on board (1,324 passengers, 899 crew).

12–13 April: Friday and Saturday
Sails through calm, clear weather, covering 2,335 km (1,451 miles).

14 April: Sunday
9.00 am: Receives an ice warning from a nearby ship, the *Caronia*. It is the first of seven ice warnings received throughout the day.
11.40 am: A Dutch liner the *Noordam* reports "much ice".
1.42 pm: Iceberg and sea-ice warning received from the *Baltic*, about 400 km (250 miles) ahead of the *Titanic*. Captain Smith is told. He tells Bruce Ismay, who puts the message into his pocket.
7.30 pm: Three ice warnings received from the *Californian*. Ice is now only 80 km (50 miles) ahead.
9.30 pm: Lookouts in the crow's nest are told to watch for icebergs.
10.00 pm: Fred Fleet and Reginald Lee start their lookout shift.
11.00 pm: *Californian* tries to warn the *Titanic* of ice but is cut off by *Titanic's* wireless operator who says: "Keep out! Shut up! You're jamming my signal."
11.39 pm: Lookouts see iceberg, 455 m (1,500 feet) ahead and sound the warning bell.
11.40 pm: *Titanic* hits iceberg.
11.50 pm: Captain Smith asks the ship's designer, Thomas Andrews, to inspect the damage.

15 April: Monday

12.00 am: Captain Smith is told the ship will sink within two hours.
12.05 am: Passengers and crew assemble on deck, ready to board the lifeboats, but there is only enough room for about half of them.
12.15 am: CQD distress signal sent.
12.25 am: *Carpathia*, 93 km (58 miles) away, heads to the rescue.
12.45 am: CQD signal changed to SOS signal. First distress rocket fired. First lifeboat lowered.
1.15 am: Bow tilts into sea.
1.30 am: Distress calls are now desperate: "We are sinking fast" and "Women and children in boats. Cannot last much longer."
2.05 am: Last lifeboat lowered. The tilt of the ship increases.
2.17 am: Last wireless message sent. Bow plunges under. Band stops playing. People jump overboard. A funnel collapses.
2.18 am: A huge roar is heard as all moveable objects crash down into the bow. The lights blink once, then go out. *Titanic* breaks in two. The bow section sinks.
2.20 am: Stern settles level for a few moments, fills with water, tilts upright, then sinks: 1,517 people drown or die of cold in the icy sea.
4.10 am: First lifeboat picked up by the *Carpathia*.
8.10 am: Last lifeboat picked up.
8.50 am: The *Carpathia* heads for New York, carrying 706 survivors.

18 April

9.00 pm: *Carpathia* reaches New York.

19 April – 25 May

United States Senate inquiry.

22 April–15 May

Ships search for bodies; 328 found.

2 May–3 July

Inquiry into the disaster by the British Board of Trade; 25,622 questions are asked. The Board recommends "more watertight compartments in ocean-going ships, the provision of lifeboats for all on board, as well as a better lookout."

14 May

A one-reel silent movie, *Saved From the Titanic, is* shown. It stars actress Dorothy Gibson, a *Titanic* survivor.

July 1980

American explorer Jack Grimm searches for the *Titanic*, but does not find the wreck.

June 1981

Jack Grimm's second unsuccessful expedition.

July 1983

Jack Grimm's third unsuccessful expedition.

1 September, 1985

A French/American expedition, led by Robert Ballard, finds the *Titanic*.

1986

Robert Ballard photographs the inside and outside of the *Titanic*.

1987

The first of more than 5,000 objects are raised from the wreck.

18 December, 1997

The film *Titanic* opens in the USA.

TITANIC FACTS AND FIGURES

Nationality: British
Cost: £1.5 million ($7.5 million)
Keel laid down: March 31, 1909
Launched: May 31, 1911
Rivets used: 3,000,000
Length: 269 m (882 ft 9 in)
Width: 28.20 m (92 ft 6 in)
Height (keel to funnel
top): 53.34 m (175 ft)
Forward mast height: 30.97 m
(101 ft 6in)
Watertight compartments: 16
Boilers: 29
Decks: 7
Propellers: 3
Funnels: 4
Top speed: 23–24 knots
Lifeboats: 16 plus 4 collapsibles
Lifeboat capacity: 1,178 people
First voyage began: 10 April, 1912
First voyage ended: 15 April, 1912
Length of service: 4.5 days
Depth of wreck: 3,798 m (12,460 ft)

Built to carry:
first-class passengers: 735
second-class passengers: 674
third-class passengers: 1,026
officers and crew: 885

Carried on maiden voyage:
first-class passengers: 329
second-class passengers: 285
third-class passengers: 710
officers and crew: 899

Died:
first-class passengers: 130
second-class passengers: 166
third-class passengers: 536
officers and crew: 685

Survived:
first-class passengers: 199
second-class passengers : 119
third-class passengers: 174
officers and crew: 214

TITANIC WEBSITES

www.keyflux.com/titanic/
Almost one million passengers have visited this site since it began in
1996. Contains a vast amount of information about the *Titanic*.

http://seawifs.gsfc.nasa.gov/titanic.html
Watch a video clip of the *Titanic* wreck site.

www.cnn.com/US/9902/21/titanic.whistle
Download the sound of the *Titanic*'s whistle.

http://216.188.92.3/~sortteam.org/mgy/
Titanic and other White Star Line ships.

www.mollybrown.com
The Molly Brown House Museum (Margaret Brown, *Titanic* survivor).

SHIPWRECK WEBSITES

General information about ships and shipwrecks:
index.waterland.net/Navis/Home/NoFrames.htm
The NAVIS project – a massive database of information on ancient ships, sites, and museums from around the world.
www.abc.se/~m10354/uwa/wreckint.htm
Worldwide shipwrecks organised into geographic regions.
www.nrc.ca/imd/ice/scdb_index.html
Database of ship collisions with icebergs.

Individual shipwrecks:
www.ocf.berkeley.edu/~mars
Atocha – a Spanish treasure ship.
www.nps.gov/vick/cairo/cairo.htm
USS *Cairo* – gunboat of the American Civil War.
www.divernet.com/wrecks/1001egypt.htm
Egypt – a diver's account of diving on the wreck of this liner.
www.hamilton-scourge.city.hamilton.on.ca
Hamilton and *Scourge* – warships sunk in Lake Ontario.
www.charlestonillustrated.com/hunley/index.html
H. L. *Hunley* – submarine of the American Civil War.
monitor.nos.noaa.gov
USS *Monitor* – ironclad of the American Civil War.

INTERNATIONAL DISTRESS CALLS

Morse Code signals:
Morse Code ceased as an official distress signal on 31 January, 1999.

CQD (—·— — —·— —··) Used from 1904. Said to be: "Come Quick Danger". Was really: "All Stations, Attention: Distress".

SOS (··· — — — ···) Replaced CQD by 1908. Said to be: "Save Our Souls" (or "Ship"). Was really no more than a distinctive set of letters.

Radio signals:
Current signals indicating a level of danger.

"Mayday! Mayday! Mayday!"
Repeated three times. From the French *m'aidez* ("help me"). Used in time of great danger.

"Pan! Pan! Pan!"
Repeated three times. From the French *panne* ("breakdown"). Used in time of lesser danger.

OTHER LOST SHIPS

The ships listed here are from all periods and come from all parts of the world. They are
listed in date order, from the oldest to the youngest. Ships described in the text are not listed.

Vessel	Date	Location	Description
Logboats	7200 BC	France	Prehistoric. Found on land. Made from hollowed-out tree trunks.
As-Sabiyah boat	5400 BC	Kuwait	Prehistoric. Found on land. The world's oldest plank-built boat.
Abydos boats	3000 BC	Egypt	Ancient Egyptian. Found on land. A fleet of 14 boats in Egypt's desert.
Khufu ships	2600 BC	Egypt	Ancient Egyptian. Found on land. Two ships buried outside the pyramid of the pharaoh Khufu.
Albenga wreck	100 BC	Mediterranean	Roman. Largest Roman cargo vessel found, with 12,000 pottery jars.
Antikythera wreck	80 BC	Mediterranean	Greek. Ship carrying a cargo of bronze sculptures, and a unique clockwork calculating device.
Lake Nemi ships	40 AD	Italy	Roman. Two of the largest ancient ships recovered. Destroyed in 1944.
Yassi Ada ship	625 AD	Aegean	Possibly Roman. Cargo ship with more than 1,100 jars of wine and oil.
Sutton Hoo ship	625 AD	England	Anglo-Saxon. Found on land. Perhaps the grave of a king.
Skuldelev ships	1080	Denmark	Viking. Five ships sunk to make a barrage across a narrow channel.
Shinan wreck	1323	Yellow Sea, Korea	Chinese. Cargo ship loaded with pottery, and seven million coins.

Vessel	Date	Location	Description
Bremen cog	1380	Germany	North European. A cargo carrier, and also a type of warship.
Newport ship	1466	Wales	North European. Found on land. Carried goods from Portugal.
Girona	1588	Irish Sea	Spanish. An Armada ship; one of the fleet sent to invade England.
Sea Venture	1609	Caribbean	English. Taking colonists to America.
Santa Margarita	1622	Atlantic	Spanish. Treasure ship.
Nuestra Señora de las Maravillas	1656	Caribbean	Spanish. Treasure ship salvaged in the 1980s.
HMS Pandora	1791	S. Pacific	British. Warship sent after mutineers who had taken over HMS *Bounty*.
HMS Agamemnon	1809	S. Atlantic	British. Warship that fought in the Battle of Trafalgar (1805).
Central America	1857	Atlantic	American. Carried 21 tonnes of gold. Salvaged in the 1980s.
Resurgam	1879	Irish Sea	British. World's first mechanically powered submarine.
Britannic	1916	Aegean	British. Sister ship of the *Titanic*. Sank after an explosion.
USS Arizona	1941	Pacific	American. Battleship sunk in attack on Pearl Harbor, in World War II.
Andrea Doria	1956	Atlantic	Italian. Liner, sank after a collision.
USS Scorpion	1968	Atlantic	American. Nuclear submarine.
Estonia	1994	Baltic	Finnish. Passenger ferry capsized and 900 drowned.
Salahuddin 2	2002	R. Meghna, Bangladesh	Bangladeshi. Overloaded ferry capsized in a storm: 300 died.

GLOSSARY

Atmospheric Diving Suit (ADS)
Diving suit that lets a diver work at
depths of up to 610 m (2,000 ft).
**Automated Underwater Vehicle
(AUV)**
Robot submersible that can stay
under water for months at a time.
Ballast
Heavy material (stone, iron) put in a
ship's hold to keep the vessel stable.
Bermuda Triangle
Area of Atlantic Ocean where ships
(and planes) have simply vanished.
Berth
Place where a ship docks (stays)
when it is in port.
Bow
The front part of a ship.
Broadside
Attack in which all the guns on one
side of a warship are fired at once.
Bulkhead
Cross-wall in the hold of ship, often
creating a watertight compartment.
Bullion
Bars of gold or silver, before being
turned into coins or other objects.
Cannon
A gun that fires cannonballs.
Cannonball
Heavy metal or stone ball.
Capsize
To overturn a ship in the water.
Cargo
Goods carried in a ship's hold.
Cog
Medieval square-sailed warship or
merchant ship of northern Europe.
Corsair
Pirate who operated in the
Mediterranean region.

CQD
An international distress call. It was
replaced by the SOS call.
Destroyer
General term for a modern warship.
Diving bell
Open-bottomed container in which a
person is lowered into deep water.
Fitting out
The time when fixtures and fittings
are put into a newly built ship.
Flotsam
Wreckage or cargo found floating
after a shipwreck.
Galleon
Large warship favoured by Spain in
the 15th and 16th centuries.
Grab
Mechanical device used by salvors to
grip and lift objects from a wreck.
Gunpowder
An explosive black powder.
Heel
To lean over to one side.
Hold
Below-deck area of ship where cargo
is stored.
Hulk
Main body part or wreck of an
old ship.
Hull
Main body part of a ship.
Human error
When a mistake by a person leads to
an accident.
Ingot
Rectangular block of metal,
especially gold or silver.
International water
Sea that is more than 19.3 km
(12 miles) from the shore.

Ironclad
Early form of warship whose hull was protected by iron plates.

Junk
Flat-bottomed sailing ship of Asia.

Keel
Bottom-most part running the length of a ship in the very centre.

Liner
Large passenger-carrying ship that sails along fixed routes ("lines").

List
Tilting of a ship in relation to the surface of the water.

Maiden voyage
A ship's very first journey.

Manifest
List of the cargo carried by a ship.

Man-of-war
Large sailing warship of the 18th and 19th centuries.

Mariner
A sailor.

Morse code
System of dots and dashes used to represent letters of the alphabet.

Piece of eight
Spanish silver coin, or piece, with a value of eight *reales*, hence its name.

Polyethylene glycol (PEG)
A type of wax used to conserve (protect) wooden objects.

Port
Left-hand side of a ship.

Ram
Bronze weapon at the front of Greek and Roman warships.

Remotely Operated Vehicle (ROV)
Submersible vehicle operated from a surface ship.

Salvage
Rescue of a wrecked or damaged ship and its cargo.

Salvor
Person who salvages a wrecked or damaged ship and its cargo

Scuttled
Deliberate sinking of a ship.

Slipway
Sloping road down which a ship slides into the water.

Snorkel
Tube which supplies surface air to a person or vessel under water.

Sonar
Device that detects underwater objects. From SOund NAvigation and Ranging.

SOS
An international distress call.

Starboard
Right-hand side of a ship.

Stern
The rear part of a ship.

Submarine
Vessel that travels under water.

Submersible
Small craft that operates under water, usually at great depths.

Territorial water
Sea that is less than 19.3 km (12 miles) from the shore.

Torpedo
Weapon that travels under water and explodes on impact with target.

Treasure-hunter
Person who searches for valuables for personal gain.

U-boat
A submarine of the German navy.

Wireless
Communication equipment used by ships to send Morse code messages.

Wrecker
Person who lures a ship ashore or who takes a ship's cargo that has been washed ashore.

INDEX

A

air-sea rescue 82, 83
Alaska 84
America 13, 51
American Civil War 52–53
Amsterdam 41
Andrea Doria 91
Andrea Gail 10
aqualung 16, 18
archaeology, marine 34–36,
    48–49, 50
Argo 28
Arizona, USS 91
Athlit Ram 47
Atlantic Ocean 10, 12, 24,
    54, 72, 76

B

Bahamas 37
Ballard, Robert 14, 27–28
Baltic Sea 56, 58
Barents Sea 32
Bass, George 35
battleships 12, 52
Bayerle, Martin 71
Beckenhouwer, Frederick 44
Bellamy, Samuel (Black
Sam) 65–66
Bermuda Triangle 12–13
Bismarck 54–55, 91
Blackbeard (Edward Teach)
    64, 65, 66
Bonny, Anne 65
Braer 84
Britannic 91
Brown, Margaret 79
Bullimore, Tony 80–81
Bulmer, Ian 59

C

Caesar, Julius 63
Cairo, USS 19
Çakir, Mehmet 35

cannibalism 77–78
cannons 47–48, 51–52,
    57–59
Caribbean Sea 64, 78, 80
Carpathia 78–79, 83
Chase, Owen 76–77
China 42–43, 47, 90
Clifford, Barry 67
coastguards 14, 82
cogs 47–48, 90
coins 30, 49, 67, 70
Cole, Isaac 77
copper ingots 34, 35
Cornwall, England 82, 84
cruise ships 68

D

Davy Jones' locker 8
Deane, John 48
distress signals 25–26,
    70, 82, 89
divers 16–18, 69
diving bells 16, 17, 58
diving suits 17, 18
Dutch East India Company
    41, 42, 45

E

Edinburgh, HMS 31–33, 36
Egypt 74–75
Egypt, ancient 30, 74, 90
environmental damage 84
escort ships 31
Estonia 91
Essex 76
Exide Challenger 80
Exxon Valdez 84

F

ferries 80, 91
fire ships 50
Fisher, Mel 38
Fleet, Frederick 25, 26
Florida 37, 38

flotsam 14, 83
fog 10, 70, 75
Franzén, Anders 59

G

Geldermalsen 40–45
General Gates 13
Gianni, Albert 75
Girona 50, 91
Glass Wreck 31
gold 8, 9, 31–33, 35, 36,
    37, 38, 74–75, 91
Greeks 30, 46–47, 63, 90
gunpowder 47
Gustav II Adolf, King of
Sweden 56–57

H

Hamilton 51–52, 58
Hansson, Sofring 58
Harland and Wolff 20, 21,
    23, 69
Hatcher, Mike 44–45
helicopters 82, 83
Henry VIII, King 48
Hood, HMS 54
Hornigold, Benjamin 66
Housatonic, USS 53–54
human error 9, 42
Humphrey, Herbert 37, 38
Hunley (submarine) 53–54
hurricanes 10, 37
Hybertsson, Henrik 57

I

ice 10–11
icebergs 11, 24, 25
ironclads 52
Ismay, Bruce 20, 79
ivory 36, 37

J, K

Japan 55
Jessop, Keith 33

jewellery 35, 36, 50
junks 30, 44
Kodima 84
Kursk 55
Kyrenia Ship 63

L

Lawrence, Ben 77
Lethbridge, John 16
lifeboat service 82, 83
liners 68–75, 91
Lloyd's 9
locating wrecks 14–16
Low, Edward 64
Lusitania 71–74
Lutine, HMS 8–9
Lutine Bell 9

M

Mary Celeste 12
Mary Rose 48–50, 58
McKee, Alexander 48
Mediterranean Sea 30, 36, 47, 63–64
Melville, Herman 76
metal detector 44
Moby Dick 76–78
Monitor, USS 52, 53
movies 10, 26, 63, 77

N

Nanking Cargo Wreck 40–45
Neptune 80
Netherlands 41, 45
Nickerson, Tom 77
North Atlantic 24, 54
North Sea 8
Nuestra Señora de Atocha 37–38
Nuestra Señora de Las Maravillas 37, 38, 91

O

oil tankers 84
Ontario, Lake 50–52
Operation Hailstorm 55

P, Q

Pacific Ocean 55
Pearl Harbor 55, 91
pirates 12, 42, 63–67
Pirrie, Lord William 20
Pompey 63–64
porcelain 30, 40–45, 90
prehistoric wrecks 90
Pulak, Cemal 35
Queen Mary II 68

R

Rackham, John (Calico Jack) 64–65
raising wrecks 19, 49, 59–60
rams 46, 47
Reade, Mary 65
Republic 70–71
rescue services 82–83
rescue ships 83
Rham, Max de 44
Rogers, Able Seaman John 9
Romans 30, 46–47, 63–64, 90
Royal Navy 8, 31
Rule, Margaret 49

S

Salamis, Battle of 46
salvage 16, 19, 32–33, 44, 48, 59, 67, 71, 75
sandbanks 8, 10
Saratoga 13
Scourge 51–52, 58
Scyllias 16–17
sea monsters 11
Seine 75
Siebe, Augustus 17
silver 8, 9, 31, 36, 37, 38, 74–75
slave ships 66
Sluys, Battle of 47
Smith, Capt. Edward 24, 26
snorkel 15
Solent 48

sonar 14
South China Seas 42
Southern Ocean 80
Spanish Armada 50, 51
Spanish galleons 31, 37
Stockholm 56–58, 60
storms 10, 13, 51, 81
submarines 31–33, 53, 55, 73, 91
submersibles 14, 18–19, 27–28
survivors 76–81
Sweden 56–60

T

teacups 40, 42
telegraph 70
Titanic 11, 14, 20–29, 69, 86–88
survivors 78–79
torpedoes 53, 54, 55, 73
treasure 6, 9, 16, 30–38, 67
treasure hunters 36–38, 44, 67, 71
Turkey 34–35

U, V

U-boats 31–32, 33, 73
Uluburun wreck 35–36
US Navy 13, 51, 55
Vasa 56–60
Vikings 90

W, Y

War of 1812 51
warships 8, 11–12, 13, 31–32, 46–55, 56–60, 91
whaling ships 76
whirlpools 13
White Star Line 20, 27, 69
Whydah 65–67
World War I 71–73
World War II 31, 54–55
wreckers 82, 84
wreck-hunters 14–19, 27
yacht racing 80–81

CREDITS

Dorling Kindersley would like to thank: Chris Bernstein for the index.
Additional photography by: Alex Wilson and Tina Chambers.

Picture Credits

The publishers would like to thank the following for their kind permission to reproduce their photographs:
a = above; b = below; c = centre; l = left; r = right; t = top.

Every effort has been made to trace the copyright holder of photographs, and we apologize for any unavoidable omissions.

3 Corbis: Lawson Wood c; 4 Corbis: Adam Woolfitt tr; 5 Corbis: Ralph White bc; 5 Mr Riddell: Marineland, France bc; 6 Corbis: Peter M Fisher bl; 7 Corbis: Jonathan Blair br; 8-9 Corbis: Ted Maheiu; 10-11 The Picture Desk: The Kobal Collection/Warner Bros 2000; 12 The Picture Desk: The Kobal Collection/ Carolco 1995 tc; 13 Corbis: John Lund; 14 Corbis: Ralph White cr; 15 Corbis: Lawson Wood; 16-17 Corbis: Jonathan Blair; 16: Charlestown Shipwreck and Heritage Centre tl; br; 18 Corbis: Ralph White; 19 Corbis: Jonathan Blair tc; 20 Mary Evans Picture Library: tr; 20 The Picture Desk: Kobal Collection/20th Century Fox/Paramount/James Cameron 1997 bc; 22 Corbis: 22 The Picture Desk: The Kobal Collection/20th Century Fox/ Paramount/ James Cameron/Merie W Wallace 1997 br; 24-25 Corbis: Denis Scott; 26-27 The Picture Desk: The Kobal Collection/20th Century Fox/ Paramount/ James Cameron/Merie W Wallace 1997; 27 Corbis: Hulton-Deutsch bc; 28 Corbis: Todd Gipstein tc; 28-29 Mr Riddell: Marineland, France; 29 Corbis: Ralph White tc; 29 Hans Jenssen: cb; 30-31 Corbis: Jonathan Blair; 30 Charlestown Shipwreck and Heritage Centre cl; 32 Corbis: Stephen Frink bl; Westlight Stock/Oz/Productions c; 33 The Picture Desk: The Kobal Collection/ Rank/Michael Powell/Emeric Pressburger 1956 cl; 34 Corbis: James Davis/Eye Ubiquitous bl; 34 National Geographic Society: Bill Curtsinger tr; 35 National Geographic Society: Bill

Curtsinger bc; 36-37 Corbis: Chase Swift bl; Jeffrey L Rotman; 38 Corbis: Jeffrey L Rotman bc; 39 Worlds Edge Picture Library; 40-41 The Bowes Museum: Abraham Storck, c1630-1710; 42-43 Corbis: Stephen Frink; 44 © Christie's Images Ltd: tr; 45 © Christie's Images Ltd: c, bl; 46 Corbis: Bettmann; 47 Ancient Art & Architecture Collection: br; 48 AKG London: br; 48 Corbis: Bettmann bkgrd; 49 Corbis: Adam Woolfitt b; Bettmann t; 50 Antiquarian Images: Hogenberg tl; 51 Corbis: Bettmann c; 52-53 Corbis: Bettmann b; 53 Daniel Dowdey: tc; 54 Hulton Archive/Getty Images; 55 Corbis: Jack Fields; 60 Corbis: Macduff Everton br; 61 Corbis: Macduff Everton; 62-63 Corbis: Douglas Kirkland; 64 Mary Evans Picture Library: tl; 65 Corbis: Joel W Rogers tr; John Springer Collection tl; 67 Corbis: Richard T Nowitz br, tl; 68-69 Corbis: Amos Nachoum; 70 Corbis: Peter M. Fisher br; 71 Hulton Archive/Getty Images; 72-73 Corbis: Bettmann; 72 Hulton Archive/Getty Images: tr; 74-75 Mary Evans Picture Library; 77 The Picture Desk: The Kobal Collection/Warner 1956; 78 Corbis: Bettmann; 79 Corbis: Bettmann br; 79 Mary Evans Picture Library: tr; 80-81 Corbis/Sygma: RAAF-Australia; bc; 82-83 Rex Features: NickSitwell; 82 Still Pictures: Mark Edwards tl; 83 Skyscan: Malcolm Bradbury tr; 84 Apex Photo Agency: bc; 86-87 Charlestown Shipwreck and Heritage Centre; 88-89 Mr Riddell: Marineland, France; 90-91 Ancient Art & Architecture Collection; 92-93 Charlestown Shipwreck and Heritage Centre.

Book Jacket Credits

Front: Rex Features: Sipa Press b. Steve Noon t.
Back: National Maritime Museum, bl. Southampton City Cultural Services tr.

All other images © Dorling Kindersley. For further information see: **www.dkimages.com**